The Ancient Indus Valley Civilization's Biggest Ci
Legacy of Mohenjo-daro, Harappa, and ̀ ̄ ̀ ̄ ̀

By Charles River Editors

Muhammad Bin Naveed's picture of Harappa's Great Hall

About Charles River Editors

Charles River Editors is a boutique digital publishing company, specializing in bringing history back to life with educational and engaging books on a wide range of topics. Keep up to date with our new and free offerings with this 5 second sign up on our weekly mailing list, and visit Our Kindle Author Page to see other recently published Kindle titles.

We make these books for you and always want to know our readers' opinions, so we encourage you to leave reviews and look forward to publishing new and exciting titles each week.

Introduction

Amy Dreher's picture of a pottery fragment found at Harappa

"Well-regulated streets (were) oriented almost invariably along with the cardinal directions, thus forming a grid-iron pattern. (At Kalibangan) even the widths of these streets were in a set ratio, i.e. if the narrowest lane was one unit in width, the other streets were twice, thrice and so on…Such a town-planning was unknown in contemporary West Asia." – B.B. Lal

When one thinks of the world's first cities, Sumer, Memphis, and Babylon are some of the first to come to mind, but if the focus then shifts to India, then Harappa and Mohenjo-daro will likely come up. These cities owe their existence to India's oldest civilization, known as the Indus Valley Civilization or the Harappan Civilization, which was contemporary with ancient Mesopotamia and ancient Egypt and had extensive contacts with the former, making it one of the most important early civilizations in the world. Spread out along the rivers of the Indus River Valley, hundreds of settlements began forming around 3300 BCE, eventually coalescing into a society that had all of the hallmarks of a true civilization, including writing, well-developed cities, a complex social structure, and long-distance trade.

Mohenjo-daro was the largest city of the Indus Valley Civilization, one of the most advanced civilizations to have ever existed, and the best-known and most ancient prehistoric urban site on the Indian subcontinent. It was a metropolis of great cultural, economic, and political importance that dates from the beginning of the 3rd millennium BCE. Although it primarily flourished between approximately 2500 and 1500 BCE, the city had longer lasting influences on the urbanization of the Indian subcontinent for centuries after its abandonment. It is believed to have been one of two capital cities of the Indus Civilization, its twin being Harappa located further north in Punjab, Pakistan.

Mohenjo-daro is an enigmatic settlement, which confuses simple definitions of what a city consists of. It has revealed little evidence of palaces, contains few definite religious buildings, and appears to have never been involved in any external or internal military conflict. The inhabitants' writing has not been deciphered, and little is known about their religious and post-mortuary beliefs. Nonetheless, the city's importance is epitomized by its monumental buildings and walls, enormous manmade platforms, innovative architectural techniques, and evidence that they engaged in trade over vast distances, with high-quality artifacts sent from the Indus Valley as far as Mesopotamia and even Africa. Of particular note was their ingenious drainage system – one of the earliest means by which sewage was drained out of the city. No other urban site of similar size had a hydraulic network as complex and effective as that of Mohenjo-daro, and it would only be surpassed thousands of years later by the network of aqueducts in Rome during the third century CE.

For centuries this city was believed to have sprung into existence suddenly and without precedent, with a highly standardized system of urban development, art, and architecture that is emulated in contemporary settlements across the Indus River Valley in a phenomenon known as the "Pan-Indus system". Although this view has changed over the last few decades, there exists no definitive hypothesis as to how they grew such a complex urban society so quickly. Fittingly, the city has an equally intriguing and mysterious narrative that explains its decline and eventual disappearance, a tale that gives the site its name: the "Hill of the Dead".

The fact that the ancient Indus Valley Civilization is also often referred to as the Harappan Civilization demonstrates how important the discovery of Harappa is. As archaeologists and historians began to uncover more of the ancient Harappa site in the 19th and early 20th centuries, a more complete picture of the city emerged, namely its importance. Research has shown that Harappa was one of the three most important Indus Valley cities, if not the most important, with several mounds of settlements uncovered that indicate building activities took place there for over 1,000 years. At its height, Harappa was a booming city of up to 50,000 people who were divided into neighborhoods by walls and who went about their daily lives in well-built, orderly streets. Harappa also had drainage systems, markets, public baths, and other large structures that may have been used for public ceremonies. Ancient Harappa was truly a thriving and vibrant city that was on par with contemporary cities in Mesopotamia such as Ur and Memphis in Egypt.

The research that has been done at Harappa over the last several decades has helped scholars understand various aspects of life there, and it has provided answers to many of the questions that had previously bewildered people about the Indus Valley Civilization. Work at Harappa has revealed that settlement was quite orderly, suggesting a strong leadership structure, but at the same time details about the ancient Harappan government itself are absent. Other discoveries show that Harappa was a very active city, where neighborhoods were subject to movement and outsiders visited regularly for trade. A series of well-built streets and walls separated the neighborhoods within Harappa and moved trade traffic in and out of the city in an orderly manner.

Perhaps most interestingly, Harappa became depopulated in the early 2nd millennium BCE as all Indus Valley cities did, but there are no signs of violent struggle, which make its collapse a mystery that remains to be solved.

Among the many cities that formed in the region was a site known today as Kalibangan, which was unknown to the modern world until archaeologists began uncovering its secrets in excavations during the 1960s. They uncovered a city that was not as large or important as the better-known sites of Mohenjo-daro and Harappa, but one that was still relatively large and the most important of all Indus cities along the now extinct Saraswati River. Excavations at Kalibangan have revealed that the city had two phases of settlement which corresponded with the two major phases of Indus Valley Civilization, and that it influenced the smaller settlements along the Saraswati River. Archaeological work at Kalibangan has also shown that although it followed some of the patterns of larger Indus cities such as Mohenjo-daro and Harappa, it was also a unique city in many ways. Kalibangan was located on a different river from the other major Indus Valley Civilization cities, and its river suffered a fate that led to the end of the city. The city of Kalibangan also presented modern archaeologists with a treasure trove of findings because it was one of the best preserved Harappan sites, giving scholars a chance to see not only how the people of Kalibangan lived, but possibly how the city died.

Once Kalibangan became depopulated after 1500 BCE for reasons that are still uncertain, its memory, or at least the memory of the Saraswati region, lived on in the epic poems of the Aryans known as the *Rig Veda*. Although the *Rig Veda* is a religious-mythological text, it can help provide some clues as to the fate of Kalibangan, including whether the Aryans were connected to the city.

The Ancient Indus Valley Civilization's Biggest Cities: The History and Legacy of Mohenjo-daro, Harappa, and Kalibangan examines the region, the civilization, and what life was like in each city thousands of years ago. Along with pictures and a bibliography, you will learn about the three cities like never before.

The Ancient Indus Valley Civilization's Biggest Cities: The History and Legacy of Mohenjo-daro, Harappa, and Kalibangan

About Charles River Editors

Introduction

Free Books by Charles River Editors

Discounted Books by Charles River Editors

The Modern Discovery of Harappa

The ancient site of Harappa is located next to the modern village of Harappa on the Pakistani side of the border in the Punjab region. It is near where the Ravi River once flowed before it changed course hundreds of years ago (Possehl 2002, 10). As British scholars fanned out across British India in the early 19th century searching for Buddhist, Sikh, and Hindu artifacts, British explorer Charles Mason first reported the site in 1826. Mason knew that the ruins were something important, but he believed they were the 4th century BCE city of Sangala, which was the capital of King Porus's empire (Possehl 1991, 6). Porus and his kingdom were of particular interest to Europeans of the time because he was the Indian king written about by the Greek historians who stood against Alexander the Great. Although Mason's discovery generated interest in Harappa, little more was done there for several decades.

In 1856, a team of British railway engineers was overseeing the construction of a railway line connecting the cities of Lahore and Multan, in what was then northern India when they unearthed a huge cache of uniform, fire-baked bricks. In flat, dry terrain, where sourcing construction materials, in particular ballast, was very difficult, this discovery saved an enormous amount of time and money. Today, just under 100 miles of track between Lahore and Karachi is laid on a bed of 4,000-year old kiln-fired bricks.

At the time, no questions were asked, and the bricks were simply quarried and used along miles of the track in either direction. As the railway edged toward the Arabian Sea, few more similar caches were unearthed, and again the bricks were simply dug up and crushed. Eventually, however, it began to dawn on some of the railway engineers that what they were dealing with was something more than simply rubble. Thus, the quarrying of the sites was halted and they were marked for future reference, but otherwise left alone.

The discovery of ancient Harappa followed a pattern similar to the discoveries made in Egypt and Mesopotamia in the 19th century in that it was led by European academics, but its discovery and subsequent excavations were also fundamentally different. Harappa was buried far beneath the ground next to the modern town of Harappa and was not even known to modern people, unlike the many sites in Egypt and Mesopotamia. In fact, Harappa was not even the subject of local legends the way the sites and monuments were in modern Egypt and Iraq. The local Hindu, Sikh, and Muslim population had no inherent hostility toward the Indus Valley Civilization the way the locals did in Egypt and Mesopotamia, but it was something they had never seen, so they never considered it positive or negative. Also unlike Egypt and Mesopotamia, it took several decades after its discovery for archaeological work to develop into an identifiable discipline. It was not until after World War II that studies became more widespread in major universities.

The first true scientific appraisal of Harappa was conducted by Alexander Cunningham in 1853 when he recorded the site's many mounds. Cunningham then developed the first extensive plans of Harappa, which were published in 1873 (Possehl 1991, 6). By the late 1800s, as Harappa was being looked at more critically and as archaeology was developing into a separate discipline, more academics began to think Harappa was something unique. Scholars knew that Harappa was probably separate from the later phases of Indian history, but they were still unsure of what it was part of, or even when it existed. Scholarship would have to wait for technology and archaeological techniques to advance.

MAJOR-GENERAL SIR ALEXANDER C. CUNNINGHAM, K.C.S.I., C.I.E.,
LATE BENGAL ENGINEERS.

Cunningham

Although Harappa and the Indus Valley civilization were opened to the world by 1899, at that time the manner of the excavation of the sites and the scholarship of the discoveries were still lagging far behind that of Egypt and the Near East. The British Viceroy of India decided to modernize the Archaeological Survey of India (ASI) by placing 26-year-old John Marshall in charge in 1899. Like most Westerners of the period, Marshall's background was in Greek and Latin, but he did acquire modern archaeological knowledge in the field under legendary archaeologist Arthur Evans in Crete (Possehl 2002, 9–10). Marshall brought new scientific methods to Indian archaeology and assigned Henry Hargreaves to investigate the mounds in

1914 (Possehl 1991, 6).

Work continued at Harappa under Hargreaves in the early 20th century, and then M.S. Vats took over the site in 1926. Vats had already successfully worked at Mohenjo-daro for quite some time, so he took what he learned at that site with him to Harappa. He would work at Harappa until the mid-1930s and then was succeeded by a number of capable archaeologists, including K.N. Sastri and Mortimer Wheeler. After a career focusing on the archaeology of Roman Britain, Wheeler became the head of the ASI in 1944. He immediately brought teams back to Harappa and began excavating Mound AB (Possehl 2002, 17–18).

Saqib Qayyam's picture of some of Wheeler's excavation work at Mohenjo-daro

In the decades after Wheeler's work at Harappa, teams from the University of California, Berkley have led many of the excavation seasons (Possehl 1991, 8–10). The totality of all the excavations have taken place over more than 36 seasons and revealed a city that was quite large and important. Houses, walls, baths, larger buildings, and cemeteries have all been discovered in the approximately 100 years of excavations at Harappa. In terms of mass, Harappa encompassed 250-500 acres and had a minimum population of 20,000 people (Possehl 2002, 66). The settlement formed slowly over a long period of time, but once it became a legitimate town, it grew quickly.

The Indus Valley Civilization

Initially, architects assumed that they were dealing with sites related to the Maurya Empire, a significant empire in ancient India that thrived between 322 BCE and 185 BCE, but soon enough it became clear that this was something much older. The archaeological discoveries around the Indus Valley Civilization revealed a Bronze Age civilization dating back to at least 3300 BCE. It had endured for perhaps 2,000 years, until about 1300 BCE. Evidence of pre-Indus Valley Civilization settlements dating back to 7000 BCE have been unearthed in Baluchistan in western Pakistan. At its peak, the known parameters of the Indus Valley Civilization covered the Indian states of Gujarat, Haryana, Punjab, Rajasthan and Jammu and Kashmir, and the Pakistani provinces of Sindh, Punjab, and Baluchistan, overlapping into parts of Afghanistan.

The Indus Valley Civilization covered an area of about 467,183 square miles. The two major sites of Mohnejo-Daro and Harappa are located in modern Pakistan, and this appears to have been the administrative center of the Indus Valley Civilization.

Com Rogues' picture of part of Mohnejo-Daro's ruins

A picture of ruins at Mohenjo-daro

That said, archaeologists quickly found that Mohenjo-daro is an enigmatic settlement defying the typically simple definitions of what a city was in antiquity. It has revealed little evidence of palaces, contains few definite religious buildings, and appears to have never been involved in any external or internal military conflict. The inhabitants' writing has not been deciphered, and little is known about their religious and post-mortuary beliefs. Nonetheless, the city's importance is epitomized by its monumental buildings and walls, enormous manmade platforms, innovative architectural techniques, and evidence that they engaged in trade over vast distances, with high-quality artifacts sent from the Indus Valley as far as Mesopotamia and even Africa. Of particular note was the ingenious drainage system, one of the earliest means by which sewage was drained out of the city. No other urban site of similar size had a hydraulic network as complex and effective as that of Mohenjo-daro, and it would only be surpassed thousands of years later by the network of aqueducts in Rome during the 3rd century CE.

For centuries this city was believed to have sprung into existence suddenly and without precedent, with a highly standardized system of urban development, art, and architecture that is emulated in contemporary settlements across the Indus River Valley in a phenomenon known as the "Pan-Indus system." Although this view has changed over the last few decades, there exists no definitive hypothesis as to how they grew such a complex urban society so quickly. Fittingly, the city has an equally intriguing and mysterious narrative that explains its decline and eventual disappearance, a tale that gives the site its name: the "Hill of the Dead."

Three phases have been identified: the "Early Harappan Phase" from 3300-2600 BCE; the "Mature Harappan Phase" from 2600-1900 BCE, and the "Late Harappan Phase" from 1900-1300 BCE. According to some estimates, the population living under the Indus Valley Civilization could have peaked at as many as 5 million. Archaeologists have also divided the lifespan of the city of Harappa into five more periods within each of the three primary periods. The Early Harappan period is known today by scholars as an era of regionalization, where specific pottery and ceramic style developed locally and then spread to other settlements (Avari 2007, 29–32). The architectural styles, such as the baths, drainage systems, and roads, were also established during the Early Harappan period, although on a much smaller scale. These innovations were then improved upon and expanded in the Mature Harappan phase.

Unlike ancient Egypt, where its three major kingdoms were separated by periods of great decline, or even ancient Mesopotamia where dynasties were often violently usurped or conquered, the phases of the Indus Valley Civilization are not separated by any great turmoil. In fact, the Indus Valley Civilization demonstrates a remarkable amount of continuity from its earliest periods until its eventual decline (Avari 2007, 30). Some cities were more adversely affected during the transitions between periods, while others, such as Harappa, show very little change. The Mature Harappan phase was generally marked by a period of great growth in the Indus Valley cities. Most of the cities grew in overall population, but also in complexity in terms of building and layout.

The Mature Harappan phase was also marked by an increase in influence of the Indus Valley cities, as illustrated by documented connections with Mesopotamian kingdoms. The Mature Harappan Indus Valley was contemporary with the Akkadian and Amorite dynasties in Mesopotamia and the Middle Kingdom in Egypt, although there is only evidence that the Harappans had direct contact with Mesopotamia. Texts from the reign of Sargon of Akkad and Gudea of Lagash describe how those Mesopotamian kings received ships from Meluhha bearing copper, stone, and gold dust. The Lagash texts offer specific details about the materials that were imported from the Indus Valley: "Many other precious materials were carried to the ensi, the builder of the Ninnu-temple: from the copper mountains of Kimash – (after) the soil had been prospected (for copper ore) – its copper was mined in clusters; gold was delivered from its mine (lit.: mountain) as dust for the ensi who wanted to build a house for his king, for Gudea they mined silver from its mine (lit.: mountain), delivered red stone from Meluhha in great amounts." (Pritchard 1992, 268).

Another section of the text describes how stones from the Indus Valley were used to construct another temple at Lagash: "When he (Gudea) was building the temple of Ningirsu, Ningirsu, his beloved king, opened up for him (all) the (trade) routs from the Upper to the Lower Sea. . . He imported (lit.: brought out) esi wood from the mountains of Meluhha and built . . . He imported nir stone and made it into a mace with three lion-heads; from the Hahhum mountains, he imported gold in dust-form and mounted with it the mace with the three lion-heads. From the mountains of Meluhha he imported gold in dust-form and made (out of it) a container (for the mace)." (Pritchard 1992, 269).

The text indicates that Lagash had extensive contact with at least one of the major Indus Valley cities, although unfortunately it cannot be said for sure if it was Harappa. Archaeological evidence recovered from the Near East corroborates the texts from Lagash and proves that the trade networks between Mesopotamia and the Indus Valley were quite extensive.

The network of trade that linked Mesopotamia and the Indus Valley also included the region of Turan (northern Persia), which was located on a plain between Mesopotamia and Meluhha. Although overland routes connected the regions, increased trade traffic during the Mature Harappan phase was facilitated by new maritime technology (Possehl 2002, 215). Overland trade routes would have connected Meluhha to Turan and Turan to Mesopotamia, but Meluhha and Mesopotamia would have been more easily connected directly via sea routs through the Indian Ocean and Persian Gulf. A number of seals from Harappa, Mohenjo-daro, and other Indus cities have been found in Kish, Ur, Susa, and Nippur, and likewise, Mesopotamian and Persian items have been excavated in the Indus Valley (Possehl 2002, 217–34), adding more proof to the idea that the Indus Valley Civilization was deeply tied to the Near East. Harappa's specific role in this ancient trade and possible geopolitical system will be considered more later, but for now it is important to understand just how extensive this system was. Evidence from Mesopotamia shows that the contacts were so extensive between the civilizations that there were even Harappan translators living in Akkad (Kuhrt 2010, 53).

The Indus Valley Civilization was much different than its counterparts in Egypt and Mesopotamia, though, because those civilizations were written about extensively by later peoples and their monuments remained to be viewed. After the Greeks and Romans had conquered those two civilizations, the monuments were still visible and a source of inspiration for numerous historians and writers. Even long after the Romans were gone and Islam became the dominant cultural force in Egypt and Mesopotamia, the monuments were still there, although some of the more zealous leaders of the new religion were resentful of the pre-Islamic civilizations. Still, those cultures were written about by Islamic scholars, even if only as "monuments of ignorance," whereas once the Indus Valley Civilization collapsed, its ruins became submerged under the rural landscape of south Asia. Generations of peasants tilled over the cities and monuments and used their bricks to construct their own buildings. Once new cultures and religions became dominant in India, only a faint conscious memory of the Indus Valley Civilization remained, with the origins of most of the elements of Indus Valley culture that were passed on having been forgotten.

The Indus Valley Civilization was a river society. As with other great river civilizations, such as those in ancient Egypt and Mesopotamia, the wealth of the society lay primarily in agriculture. Key to survival was the ability to harness the seasonal inundation, both for irrigation and transport, but also for an annual deposit of fresh alluvial soils. Trade was also a significant pillar of the Indus Valley economy, and trade networks were extensive, stretching as far afield as Central Asia, Mesopotamia, the Arabian Peninsula and the Persian Gulf.

The Indus Valley Civilization developed one of the earliest known written languages, standardized across its entire geographic scope. The Indus script, also known as the Harappan script, is dated to the Mature Harappan Period that existed between 3500 BCE and 1900 BCE. Known examples of Indus script take the form of symbols, or hieroglyphs, which are uniformly short in length. In the absence of any bilingual versions, the Indus script remains one of the very few undeciphered forms of ancient writing. As a result, what is known about the Indus Valley Civilization is drawn from extant written texts, as well as archaeology and educated guesses. As with all of the major Harappan sites, the name the ancient Harappans gave to Kalibangan remains a mystery. The name "Kalibangan" is derived from a nearby settlement, and the city is also sometimes referred to as "Kal Vangu" or "Philibangan" (Possehl 2002, 74).

What the archaeological evidence does reveal is that the various civic establishments and municipalities that make up the urban structure of the Indus Valley were highly organized and regulated. Most displayed common, standardized, and recognizable features. This implies a strong centralization, a uniform system of construction, and a regime of code enforcement. A style of urban and rural separation is suggested by evidence of a rural economy centered on agriculture and livestock and an urban economy focusing on manufacturing, arts and crafts. Trade, of course, was an outlet for Indus crafts, and indeed, artefacts of Indus manufacture have been found in widely dispersed locations.

Urban life appears to have been extremely sophisticated for the period, with evidence of indoor plumbing, systems of human waste removal, and bathing facilities, which historians frequently remark were superior in many cases to those found in modern Indian homes. Public baths and public toilets were present in the cities of the Indus Valley long before they appeared in Rome, all of which, notwithstanding the extraordinary social achievement, hints also at a preoccupation with cleanliness and purity.

This, in turn, has led to much speculation on the spiritual and religious practices of the Indus Valley Civilization, leading religious scholars to speculate that some of the earliest elements of Hinduism found their expression here during this period. Purity and cleanliness of body play a central role in modern Hinduism, as does ritual bathing. As a consequence, archaeologists and historians have speculated that the elegant and sophisticated bathing and ablution facilities in many Indus Valley sites are a reflection of an early version of Hinduism.

The various Indus Valley sites have also uncovered countless objects and artefacts to further intrigue and perplex archaeologists. Some of the most interesting of these are hundreds of tiny soapstone seals used to inscribe symbols and designs in soft clay. They have been identified as most likely pertaining to trade, and to methods of marking property. Similar seals have been unearthed as far afield as Mesopotamia, all displaying an identical array of symbols, which tends to confirm the existence of a sophisticated trade relationship between the two societies.

While the use of the seals is easy to infer, and trade is the most reasonable inference, the significance of the various symbols is much less clear. The vast majority of the seals portray male animals with prominent horns and well-defined flanks. Some are recognizable while others are clearly mythic. In general, it appears that any male artistic portrayal takes the form of an animal, while the representation of the female form is almost always literal, but exaggerated. Comparisons have been drawn between these and the ancient Venus representations originating from Europe, which implies an interest in reproduction, potency, and fertility. The most common image represented on the seals is a "unihorned" bull, which, along with highly sexualized portrayals of women, all tend to support this. There can be no doubt, therefore, that sexuality and fertility were central to the culture and religion.

Another striking feature of the urban society, often remarked upon by historians, was the highly sophisticated urban design and architecture. This, as mentioned already, included public baths and toilets, but also many other features of an advanced urban society, replicated only much later in other notable urban societies. This quality of urban planning and architecture implies strong and efficient municipal government, which in turn speaks of strong and clearly defined central government.

Granaries, harbors and docks, sophisticated river transit, and communications with the coast, alongside flood control and levies, are all features of some of the sites, indicating a highly developed and sophisticated civilization. What is not evident, however, is monumental construction, which was the case in Egypt, and there certainly appears to be no evidence of palaces or temples.

All of this leads to the question of how the Indus Valley Civilization was organized, administered and ruled. Nothing in the archaeological record offers any definitive answer, other than perhaps the fact that strong, centralized authority certainly did exist. This can be determined from the uniformity of civic structure, with details as diverse as civic planning and the size of standard construction bricks. There are intriguing clues, however, such as the apparent uniformity of wealth distribution, which historians have speculated suggests an egalitarian society without hereditary and absolute leadership.

This is most evident in death and burial. There is an indication of established burial practice that feature numerous ordinary interments, but no lavish or ostentatious sites or memorials to great kings and priests. This does not prove or even suggest that the society was without powerful rulers, for it is quite possible that noble burial rites were different, with cremation as a possibility. Still, the lack of visible memorials to powerful men and great rulers is certainly unusual for the ancient world.

There is also no specific reference to war, from which one might surmise that the society was peaceful, or perhaps simply that it was politically united and thus not at war with itself. It is also true that without powerful outside forces to interfere with the development of the civilization or challenge it, there was no one to fight and no one to defend against.

All of this paints a picture of a highly accomplished society, and certainly one ahead of its time in many respects. It was a society concerned with reproduction and fertility. The objects of religious veneration were probably certain male animals associated with virility, most notably the bull. Female powers of reproduction are also frequently represented. Evidence of meditation and of purification rites again hint at an early version of Hinduism, and a preoccupation with the balance of life and nature, and of reproduction and renewal. The longevity of the Indus Valley society and evidence of its continuity suggest a degree of entrenched conservatism, and an environment of apparent wealth and plenty.

The Indus Valley Civilization covered a huge region, but its trade practices meant that that coastal communities and ports were particularly important. The Gujarat region of India is defined almost entirely by the Saurashtra region, or the Kathiawar peninsula. It is bordered to the north by Pakistan and the state of Rajasthan, to the east by Madhya Pradesh and in the south by Maharashtra. During the existence of the Indus Valley Civilization, the region of Gujarat formed the southernmost provinces, and today Gujarat is home to 13 listed Indus Valley sites. Some are quite obscure, but perhaps the most famous are Lothal, Dholavira and Gola Dhoro.

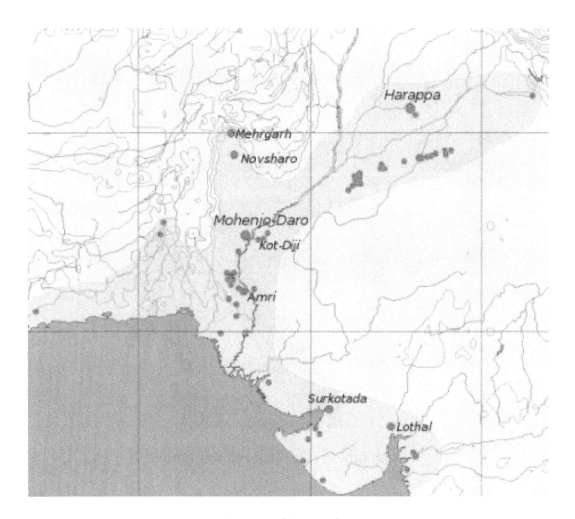

A map of the region

A picture of excavated ruins at Lothal

Of these, Lothal is perhaps the most interesting, simply because it was the principal seaport of the entire Indus Valley Civilization. Its ruins are located about 20 miles southwest of modern Ahmedabad, at the northern end of the Gulf of Khambhat. The site was first discovered in 1954, after the partition of India, in a series of excavations undertaken by the Archaeological Survey of India. To the north of Lothal, at the tip of the Gulf of Kutch, lies another significant port, Surkotada. Somewhat smaller than Lothal, Surkotada is notable for the discovery of horse remains, the only instance of such remains being found. Surkotada was established as a settlement in the later phase of the Indus Valley Civilization, and it was populated for about four centuries without any major breaks or abandonment.

Bernard Gagnon's picture of an excavated well and bathroom at Lothal

Another important site is Dholavira, located on an isolated island, Khadir Bet, on the salt plains of Rann of Kachchh, close to the current border with Pakistan. The site was unearthed in the 1960s as part of the same Archaeological Survey of India program that discovered Lothal, and numerous other catalogued and numbered sites all along the coast, and in the interior. Dholavira has been in almost continuous excavation since it was first discovered, and some of the unique features of the city are its uniform planning and a series of water reservoirs, all surrounded by heavy fortifications. These, in combination with the location of the settlement on an island in what is now a salt pan, suggest the need for defense.

Lalit Gajjer's picture of ruins at Dholavira

A picture of one of Dholavira's reservoirs

Dholavira was obviously extremely dry, because a total of 16 reservoirs lie in and around the settlement. They offer more evidence of civic planning, but also proof of the high level of engineering expertise necessary to manage water supplies in such a sophisticated way. As mentioned earlier, the usual haul of seals, graves, and inscriptions all indicate that the Gujarati sites of the Indus Valley Civilization were centers of trade, agriculture, and craft. As such, they were probably wealthier and more sophisticated than the settlements in the interior, simply because of their proximity to the coast and the advantages of trade and interaction with other cultures. What this says about Gujarat as a region, even during its earliest history, was that it was the main center for trade and commerce, which remains the character of the region to the present day.

The Indus Valley Civilization began to slip into decline around 1800 BCE, and as with so much else about this civilization, the reasons for this are unclear. In the 20th century, the most persuasive theory speculates that the Indus Valley was overrun by light-skinned, Aryan races originating from central and western Asia who eventually deposed the darker skinned Indus dwellers. More recent scholarship, however, suggests that the Aryan invasion was something less than an invasion, and more of a gradual assimilation. By the time the Aryans began arriving in the region in significant numbers, around 1600 BCE, the Indus Valley Civilization was already in decline. Other theories, perhaps more plausible, suggest climate change and alterations in the course of the Indus River. Whatever the case, by 1600 BCE, settlements were being abandoned, and the population was tending to migrate east in the direction of the Ganges Valley.

If the Aryans arrived as a migration rather than an invasion, they coexisted for a time, without necessarily integrating with the darker skinned original inhabitants. The Aryan question is a very difficult one, not only because of the Nazi appropriation of the history and symbolism of Aryan predominance, but also because of the idea that the Aryans introduced the progenitor of Hinduism into India, which would imply that Hinduism is not a truly representative Indian institution. That would never be an easy fact for Hindu nationalists to accept, and indeed, many will not accept it.

By 1300 BCE, the Indus Valley Civilization had largely disappeared, although elements of its urban culture remained to be absorbed into a new social order. That said, when the cities were depopulated, sometime in the early to mid-second millennium BCE, they were not reoccupied, so time and the environment took their toll, along with the increasing population on the Indian subcontinent. The growing population needed more land for cultivation and housing, which meant that eventually any sign of the Harappan Civilization was lost.

However, in the early 19th century, while India was under British rule, a new class of scholars fanned out across the land to study the ancient sites. These early British scholars, who were influenced by the Enlightenment and were like other archaeologists studying the ruins of Egypt and Mesopotamia at that time, had a great respect for premodern India, especially its Hindu and Buddhist past. These early Western scholars of the pre-Modern Near Eastern and Far Eastern worlds became known as "Orientalists," as their studies related to anything ancient and to the east of the Hellenic world, including Egypt.

Within the first couple of decades of the 19th century, several sub-disciplines within the Orientalist field began to develop. Egyptologists were those who studied ancient Egypt, Assyriologists covered most of ancient Mesopotamia and Persia to some extent, and Indology referred to the study of ancient Indian culture and languages. Max Müller (1823-1900), a German, was a pioneer in the field of Indology, translating many formerly obscure Sanskrit texts, but given that India was a British colony in the 1800s, most of the early Indologists were British and their focus was on the archaeological sites left by the Aryans. Later, in terms of physical culture, language and religion, the interest revolved primarily around Sanskrit and the early Vedic, Hindu and Buddhist religions. India had a wealth of materials for these early Indologists to work with, from obscure texts hidden away in monasteries and temples to monuments that had been reclaimed by time and war.

As these British scholars were searching for overlooked Buddhist sites in the Indus River Valley, they discovered the ruins of Harappa, and then Mohenjo-daro, in 1924 (Avari 2007, 40-42). The earliest surveys of those sites gave way to excavations in the region and the eventual realization that an entirely new civilization had been discovered that pre-dated any other culture in India. In fact, by the middle of the 20th century, scholars had determined that the Harappan Civilization, as it came to be known after the first city to be discovered, was contemporary with the first civilizations of Egypt and Mesopotamia.

Unlike ancient Egypt and ancient Mesopotamia, where the end of dynasties brought drastic declines in central authority, culture and the standard of living, this was not the case for the Harappan Civilization. It was once believed that the Early and Mature Harappan cultures were distinct, but in recent decades Indus scholars have recognized the continuity of traditions that carried over from the two periods (Avari 2007, 30). The major difference, though, was that the culture of the Mature Harappan was more extensive and complex, and the cities were larger and more developed. There is more evidence of writing, monumental architecture, science, art, long-distance trade and an early global system.

Many of the essential elements of the Mature Harappan Civilization still remain a mystery to modern scholars. One of the most enduring questions is whether the Harappan culture was ever a unified empire, which would have been in the Mature Harappan Period if at all, or if it was instead a collection of city-states, similar to different periods in Mesopotamian history and the Maya in Mesoamerica. The grid pattern of the streets in the largest Harappan cities and similar overall structure has led many scholars to assume a central authority or influence and in the least suggests "a high degree of competency in management and administration by those in authority" (Avari 2007, 45). The idea is that the uniformity of the cities either began in one, or just a few of the major cities, and then spread consciously to other cities. The other theory is that the major cities of Mohenjo-daro and Harappa may not have consciously spread the grid pattern of street building to other cities, but that the other cities were so connected with the larger cities through trade that they deliberately adopted the style.

The size of the Harappan cities unfortunately does not help clear up the issue. Mohenjo-daro, Harappa and Ganwerilwala, the three largest Harappan cities, may have had as many as 40,000 inhabitants each, while cities in the next tier of size, which include Kalibangan, had at least 1,000 inhabitants. The numbers of the largest cities are comparable to cities in Mesopotamia and Egypt at the time, but do not necessarily make an argument for or against a unified kingdom or empire. The three major cities may have been capitals of regional empires, with Kalibangan and other cities of similar size being provincial capitals (Haywood 2005, 76). Whether or not the Harappan cities were part of a unified empire or regional capitals may never be known, but the complexity of the layout of those cities is certain.

The largest cities, and even some of the small Indus villages, featured street layouts according to the cardinal directions. This has led many modern scholars to conclude that the Indus cities' grid patterns were related to astronomy, which in turn was related to their religious beliefs (Kenoyer 1999, 52). This theory is quite logical when one consider the sacred role that architecture played in the Bronze Age. The contemporary pyramids of Egypt and the ziggurats of Mesopotamia were both connected to those cultures' ideas of the celestial bodies and their roles in religion, but there is no evidence indicating that those cultures built streets or roads that were

21

somehow connected to the heavens. With that said, neither the Egyptians nor the Mesopotamians built streets that were as perfectly laid out on a grid pattern as the Indus streets were. City streets in ancient Egypt and ancient Mesopotamia seem to have evolved more organically, following what were sometimes circuitous routes. They were not clearly planned as the streets in the Indus Valley cities were. The question of the symbolism of the Indus Valley cities' grid pattern streets raises the even bigger question about the nature of the Harappans' religion.

There are a number of archaeological clues that help possibly outline the Harappans' religion, some of which are from Kalibangan. Religious scholars, historians, and anthropologists have also identified a number of elements in the later Vedic and Hindu religions that may have originated in the Indus Valley, but much of this remains conjecture (Avari 2007, 48). No temples have been positively identified in any of the Indus cities, although many believe a large one was discovered in Mohenjo-daro (Kenoyer 1999, 62), and scholars are not certain what is religious among the plethora of smaller items that have been discovered at the numerous Harappan sites. Some of the most common smaller items discovered at Indus Valley excavations are seals. Seals were commonly used in ancient times by royalty and other powerful people to send official messages and other items. As such, seals had great authority and were sometimes displayed with religious motifs. Unicorns were common on many Indus seals, indicating that they may have been mythological animals that were venerated (Kenoyer 1999, 18).

Some Harappan seals show a possible Mesopotamian influence, while others appear to show scenes of religious rituals that are known from the Hindu religion (Kenoyer 1999, 114). A well-known seal from Mohenjo-daro features a figure seated in a "yogi" position, which many scholars think is an example of a religious symbol (Kenoyer 1999, 113). The "Shiva" seal and the potential references to religious rituals on the other seals has led some scholars to see a fair amount of religious continuity from the Harappan culture to later periods in Indian history. The yogi seal also has writing on it, which would no doubt be helpful in understanding the Harappan religion if it could be deciphered, but unfortunately no one has yet been able to crack the Indus code.

The Indus Valley Civilization possessed all the hallmarks to meet the classical definition of a civilization, including a written language. Archaeologists have identified more than 4,200 inscribed objects, with most coming from Mohenjo-daro and Harappa, but a sizable number have also been discovered in Kalibangan. The written language has 419 known signs, but it has yet to be deciphered (Avari 2007, 50-51). Scholars believe that due to the number of characters in the Indus language, it was most likely a logosyllabic or logoconsonantal written language, similar to the ancient Egyptian language, but unlike the ancient Egyptian language there is no known script that accompanies it. The ancient Egyptian hieroglyphic script remained unknown until the Rosetta Stone was discovered in the late 18th century, but so far, all known examples of the Indus script have been found alone. If the Indus script is ever deciphered, the world would know much more about the Harappans' religion, as well as the ethnic identity of the Harappan people. Many historians believe that the Harappans were of Dravidian ethnicity (Haywood 2005, 76), but that theory raises more questions than it answers. If the Harappans were Dravidians, and if they migrated into southern Indian where most of the Dravidian people have lived for centuries, it's not clear why they didn't carry elements of the Harappan culture with them.

Writing gave the Harappans the ability to develop a sophisticated culture that had far-ranging influence, but it was not enough to stop the ultimate collapse of the civilization. The final phase of the Indus Valley Civilization was known as the Late Harappan or Post-Urban phase. The Post-Urban term refers to the abandonment or severe depopulation of nearly every city in the Indus Valley (Possehl 2002, 237). Some of these cities, such as Harappa, continued to exist as settlements, but they were shadows of their former selves and could not be considered cities by any definition. Some sub-regions within the Indus Valley did better than others during this period: the Punjab, which includes Harappa, survived the period better, although it too saw its urban areas reduced. Possehl notes that after the Late Harappan phase ran its course, the settlement patterns in the Indus Valley essentially returned to what they were in the late Neolithic Period (Possehl 2002, 237).

The demise of the Indus Valley Civilization and the ancient city of Harappa likely went hand-in-hand. As Harappa fell, so too did the other cities in the civilization, although at different rates since some cities held on longer than others. Eventually, though, the entire Indus Valley Civilization was subsumed by the countryside, and its once great cities were forgotten for over 3,000 years. Although scholars once believed that the Aryan migrations around 1500 BCE played a major role in the collapse, there is actually very little archaeological evidence of widespread destruction in the cities (Kenoyer 1999, 19). Thus, scholars now believe that there were a number of factors that contributed to the downfall of the Indus Valley Civilization, many of them local. Overextended economic and political networks certainly played a role, especially after some of the river began drying up and the Indus shifted course (Avari 2007, 53). But even after the Indus Valley Civilization collapsed, many of its technologies, architectural styles, and religious ideas were continued by later Indian cultures, thereby ensuring that the Indus Valley Civilization would have a long and enduring influence on the world.

Early Harappan Harappa

Like the ancient Egyptian and Mesopotamian cultures, the ancient Harappan culture did not just develop immediately. It formed over a longer period of time during the Neolithic Period, and the presence of the Indus and the other rivers in the valley were a prerequisite for growth because they allowed the people of the Indus Valley to expand farming and travel throughout the valley. By the early 4th millennium BCE, the people of the Indus Valley began to coalesce around particular locations, and the early signs of the Harappan Civilization began to form. Settlement of the area near ancient Harappa began around 3800 BCE (Possehl 2002, 66), but it was not until between 2800 and 2600 BCE that the settlement became a town, which was near the end of the Early Harappan phase.

Harappa was quite modest in size during this phase, growing to about 62 acres (Kenoyer 1999, 49). Although it was not very big at this point in history, it was relatively large compared to the other sites in the Indus Valley, and it was also during this period when the first signs of the unique Harappan culture were manifested.

The street layout of Early Harappan Harappa was similar to that in Mohenjo-daro during the same period, but instead of a rigid grid pattern, as the streets of the Indus Valley cities are so often described, they were more of an "irregular net plan" (Kenoyer 1991, 34). What this means is that instead of a typical modern grid pattern (as the Harappan street pattern is often erroneously described), the streets went in straight lines, but often took angles of the shortest distance between two points. Streets were obviously used for transportation, but along with the walls, they were also used to segregate different neighborhoods of the city.

Early Harappan Harappa also featured wells, drainage systems, and baths, similar to Mohenjo-daro, although the baths at Harappa were smaller and less elaborate. The dwellings in both cities were made of mudbrick in the Early Harappan phase, but due to the nature of modern settlement patterns, though, locating and identifying the different historical phases of Harappa's existence has not been easy (Kenoyer 1991, 34).

Much of the area around ancient Harappa is used for agricultural purposes today, so archaeologists have been forced to dig in limited areas and have only uncovered a fraction of the ancient city. Thankfully, though, there were enough excavations completed by the late 20th century for scholars to determine in what areas the first settlements began. A mound that was labeled "Mound E" by Vats is now believed to be the site of the first Early Harappan settlement at Harappa (Kenoyer 1991, 40).

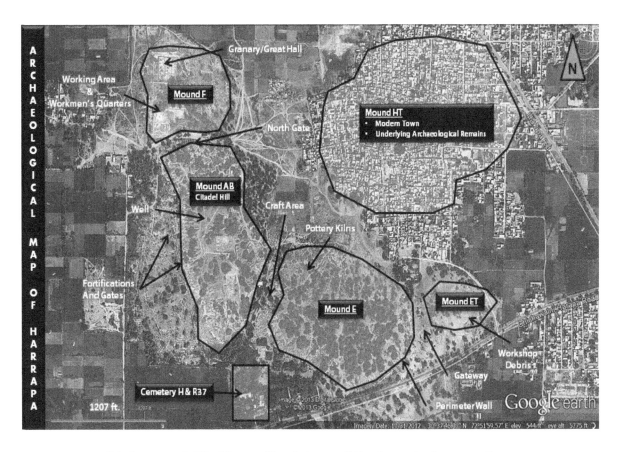

Muhammad Bin Naveed's picture of the layout of excavations

Once settlers began to build on Mound E, the city of Harappa grew rapidly, and it became one of the three preeminent locations in the Indus Valley. There were likely several reasons for Harappa's quick growth in the early 3rd millennium BCE, several of which will probably never be known, but archaeologists familiar with the site and other ancient Indus Valley cities point to its location as a primary reason. Harappa was located on the crossroads that connected the western highland and northern plains to the Ghaggar-Hakra Valley and the southern plains (Kenoyer 1991, 57). This location made travel to and from the city relatively easy, and it was also a central location between different sub-regions of the Indus Valley. Due to these factors, Harappa was in a prime location for long-distance trade, and evidence of the trade that flowed through Early Harappan Harappa can be found in a number of places in the archaeological record.

Among Harappa's many noticeable features are its walls, which were built throughout all phases of its existence. In the case of most ancient cities, walls were usually used to prevent or mitigate attacks from outsiders. In some places, such as ancient Egypt, walls were used to separate the sacred from the profane in temples, but at Harappa its many walls do not appear to have functioned in either manner. None of the Harappa walls show signs of damage from battle, and they do not appear to have been directly associated with any temples or religious functions.

Without evidence of a religious or military function, one historian pointed out that the walls could have demonstrated a complex social organization on the part of Harappa's city planners (Kenoyer 1999, 470). The walls separated different residential neighborhoods, which were apparently segregated by social class. Just as important as segregating the different classes of Harappan society, Kenoyer believes that the walls were also used to control trade and commerce (Kenoyer 1999, 56). Given that Harappa was vital for trade, the permanent population of the city would have been augmented on any day by hundreds or even thousands of merchants from other cities in the Indus Valley, as well as merchants from southern India, the Iranian Plateau, and even Mesopotamia. These non-residents would have been efficiently funneled through the city not only via the streets, but also by the walls, which would have kept the merchants from wandering through residential neighborhoods.

When Mortimer Wheeler conducted his excavations at Harappa during the 1940s, he was intrigued by the walls, especially when he determined that they had not suffered any major attack. Wheeler formulated a theory about the walls which has since been advocated by other archaeologists such as Kenoyer: the gateways of Harappa actually combined religious and trade elements. According to this theory, the gateways of Harappa's walls were "part of an elaborate ceremonial or ritual entry to the city rather than for defensive purposes" (Kenoyer 1991, 35).

All of the archaeological evidence indicates that the trade taking place at Harappa was extensive, and that while plenty of materials left the city, some were finished there and remained in Harappa as well. Stones and other raw materials used for monument building would have passed through Harappa on their way to other Indus Valley cities and ultimately Mesopotamia (although the text from Lagash cited earlier did not mention any cities within Meluhha, due to Harappa's size it is safe to assume that some of those raw materials left Harappa for Mesopotamia). In return, carnelian for beads, as well as chert, which has a variety of uses, would have proceeded to Harappa to be used in the local workshops. Copper was also imported to the city for tools, along with seashells for ornaments (Kenoyer 1999, 49).

Mature Harappan Harappa

Early Harappan Harappa clearly developed into a large, influential city that was full of life, but as the city grew, so too did problems associated with growth, such as sanitation. This meant that the physical focal point of the city would also have to change.

The Mature Harappan phase of the Indus Valley Civilization began around 2600 BCE in most sub-regions of the valley, and it was marked by intensive urbanization throughout the Indus Valley, albeit with a fair amount of cultural continuity from the Early Harappan phase. Unlike the contemporary civilizations in Egypt and Mesopotamia, there was no widespread collapse between these two phases of Harappan culture; in most places, it was more of a gradual transition, and at Harappa, the transition was marked by the physical movement of a large part of the population.

Modern excavations at Harappa eventually shifted from Mound E to "Mound F," and this site was later determined to be the core of Mature Harappan Harappa. Construction on this section of Harappa began during the transition from the Early to the Mature Harappan phase, or sometime around 2600 BCE (Possehl 2002, 66). There are no signs that Harappa suffered any destruction due to war or natural disasters, so it seems the focal point of the city moved due to a number of other factors. Proper waste disposal probably played some role, with historians suggesting that as garbage began to pile up in and around Mound E, the people moved their primary living quarters. The growing population of the city also meant that more houses and facilities were needed, so a move was made to an area with more space.

Among some of the new building features discovered on Mound F were parallel walls that ran alongside either side of one of the major roads, which terminated at a large building once believed to be a granary (Possehl 2002, 66). The possible functions of this granary will be discussed more later, but it is important to note that many of the major buildings during this period were constructed with bricks. During the Early Harappan phase, the Harappans used mudbricks exclusively to build most of their walls, houses, and major buildings. Mudbricks were widely used in the ancient world because the workers needed few tools or material to make them, and once the bricks were made from mud and a form, they could simply be put into place. Mudbrick structures could be fairly stable, but they did need to be regularly maintained and sometimes entirely rebuilt.

At the beginning of the Mature Harappan phase, things began to change when the process of baking bricks in kilns was introduced to the Indus Valley. The walls continued to be built primarily from mudbrick, but baked brick facings were added to them in the Mature Harappan phase (Kenoyer 1999, 55).

The largest (and therefore presumably the most important) of all the structures is the so-called granary on Mound F, whose ruins indicate it played a central role in Mature Harappan Harappa. The massive rectangular structure was made of mudbrick with a wooden superstructure, but today only the foundation primarily remains. The building was comprised of two rows of six rooms that were about 50 by 20 feet (Kenoyer 1999, 64). The overall size and large open rooms in this building led Vats to believe it was a granary. In 1946, when Wheeler was conducting excavations at Harappa, he discovered what he believed was a large wooden mortar in the center of a brick platform near the granary. When he made the discovery, wooden mortars were still used in many parts of the world to remove husks from grain, so Wheeler believed the discovery confirmed Vats' initial theory (Kenoyer 1999, 65).

Later scholars have pointed out, though, that no evidence of grain has been recovered from the building, leading many to believe it served a different function. Kenoyer and others believe that the granary was actually used for state or religious functions, pointing to the seals and other inscriptions that were excavated from its foundation (Kenoyer 1999, 65). Others have looked to the Harappans' contemporaries in Egypt and Mesopotamia for a potential clue as to the function of the granary, and they believe it very likely could have been a temple. In Mesopotamia and Egypt, temples served as both religious and administrative centers, with the rooms inside divided according to use. The various rooms would seem to follow this pattern, as some would have been dedicated to sacred functions while others were reserved for affairs of the state.

As discussed earlier, Mound E was the site of the earliest ancient Harappan settlement, and after the city grew and transitioned into the Mature Harappan phase, the major development of the settlement moved to Mound F and Mound ET, but Mound E was also inhabited. Both mounds are at the southern end of the ancient Harappa settlement and are delineated by a modern road. The Mature Harappan level of excavation on mounds E and ET has revealed that the trade activity that began in the Early Harappan phase had grown even more and had become the major industry of the city, driving its growth.

The remains of an outer wall at the Mature Harappan level were discovered just south of both mounds (Possehl 2002, 66). As with the walls discovered in other parts of Harappa, this wall apparently functioned to move traffic and to keep neighborhoods segregated instead of for any defensive purposes. The mudbrick wall was fairly wide at 30-35 feet thick in some parts (Kenoyer 1999, 55), which would have been imposing even if it had been intended for defensive purposes.

The southern wall had a large gateway that probably opened into the city's main market area, which demonstrates the importance of trade to the people of Harappa (Kenoyer 1999, 55). The walls and the gate would have funneled all outsiders to where they needed to go, while keeping them from disturbing the permanent residents of the city.

The streets of Mature Harappan Harappa were wide and orientated to the cardinal directions in the same pattern that was mentioned earlier. Running along the streets were a series of drains that would have carried rain and waste, and the drainpipes, which were made of baked brick, were connected to each other in a pattern that mirrored those of the streets (Kennoyer 1991, 51). The well-known Harappan bathing platforms were connected to the drains, as were many of the private homes, which actually had latrines. Some of the bigger homes were equipped with sump pots that connected to drains that in turn emptied into the city's main drainage system. The drains that connected the private homes to the system were open, while the larger ones they connected to in the central city were closed and buried under the main streets. A sequence of four drains exited the city outside of the main gateway for Mound E and Mound ET onto the outlying plain. Sump pits were located in regular intervals along the main sewage drains, which had to be cleaned out on a regular basis (Kenoyer 1999, 60–62).

Despite the mess that would have been apparent from the city's drainage system just south of the wall, excavations have uncovered houses and bathing platforms from the Mature Harappan phase. Kenoyer believed that this area served as temporary housing for the out-of-town merchant caravans (Kenoyer 1999, 55), which would make sense in some ways. After all, this would mean the outsiders, not the local Harappans, had to deal with the stench from the drainage system runoff. It would stand to reason that since Harappa was so active in trade and that many merchants from other cities and even other lands outside of the Indus Valley would have visited the city, the temporary guests would have been given the least desirable real estate. That said, the existence of bathing platforms suggests that a significant portion of the "out-of-town" merchants were from other Indus Valley cities that shared similar cultural and religious beliefs with the people of Harappa. If the baths were of significance for rituals or religious purposes, and if they were not used exclusively for hygienic purposes, then they would have only been important to other Indus Valley merchants. Merchants from Mesopotamia and Persia would have viewed the baths as a novelty and a religious type of temple that they probably would not have gone near.

Just to the east of Mound E is Mound ET. Much less work has been done on this mound, but houses have been discovered, leading archaeologists to believe that it was a "suburb" of the main city (Kenoyer 1999, 55). Of course, the term suburb does not necessarily mean the same thing as it does today, only that it was a newer development that was physically apart from the earlier, planned development of Harappa. The city and its growth may have been planned to a certain extent by its leaders (although there is no evidence of this), but even if so, as Harappa became a major economic and possibly religious center, its growth extended beyond what would have been planned or envisioned. Mound ET then was either a haphazard attempt by the city's leaders to deal with this growth, or it was constructed by individuals apart from the government. As such, it did not have the complex drainage system and baths that were found in other parts of earlier phases of Harappa.

Just to the west of Mound E are ancient Harappa's two cemeteries. Designated Cemetery R-37 and Cemetery H, they contain human remains from the Mature and Later Harappan periods, with R-37 being the Mature Harappan cemetery and H being the Late Harappan cemetery. In the absence of readable Indus texts, scholars are left to rely solely on archaeology to understand details about Harappan religion, and in such cases, the nature of burials can reveal much about a society. For instance, if any artifacts are discovered in burials, then ideas about the afterlife and social stratification become clearer.

Cemetery R-37 is so named for the excavation square where it was discovered by Sastri in the 1937–38 excavation season. After making his discovery that year, Sastri continued to excavate Cemetery R-37 for the next four seasons, and the workers unearthed a trove of important archaeological information about the Indus Valley in general and Harappa specifically (Possehl 1991, 8). Work on Cemetery R-37, along with other Indus Valley cemeteries, revealed that it is, so far, the largest of all known Mature Harappan cemeteries (Possehl 2002, 66). Although only a small portion of the cemetery has been excavated, it is believed to be no larger than 164 feet by 164 feet (Possehl 2002, 169), which is still quite considerable. As excavations after Sastri indicated that the cemetery was larger than previously believed, it was subdivided into sections named R-37A and R-37C.

Most of the human remains recovered from Cemetery R-37 were incomplete, but careful examination of those pieces indicates that they belonged to nearly 200 different individuals. Of the samples whose sex could be definitively determined, 84 were female and 57 were men, with the majority being between the ages of 17 and 55 (Possehl 2002, 170).

The graves of the deceased were not especially ornate, but they did involve a certain amount of technical knowledge and resources to construct. All of the deceased were interred in a north-south orientation, which indicates some sort of religious symbolism, but without more knowledge of the Indus Valley religion, it is difficult to say for sure. The orientation may have been related to the Indus River, which generally flows in a northeast to southwest direction. It would be logical to think that the Indus River played a major role in Harappan religion the way the Ganges does today in India, and that the positions of the burials could represent some ethereal journey, but this would still be guessing.

Some of the graves were lined with baked bricks, while in others the remains were placed in wooden coffins. Nearly all of the deceased were buried with ornaments from daily life, such as copper artifacts and beads, but only the females were interred with shell bangles (Possehl 2002, 169).

Among some of the more interesting and useful items discovered in Cemetery R-37 were several pottery vessels and clay and animal figurines. For archaeologists and anthropologists, pottery is often used to determine a particular group's ethnic background or the chronological period when it was made. Much of the pottery recovered from Harappa was in shards, as would be expected of vessels more than 4,000 years old, but most of the complete vessels found at Harappa were recovered from Cemetery R-37 (Dales 1991, 62). A number of small clay figurines were also found in Cemetery R-37, although most were not directly in the burial pits. The figurines were animal and human and were discovered in a thick layer of ancient debris on top of the cemetery, which, combined with the fact that none were found directly in graves, does not suggest they were used for rituals or religious purposes (Dales 1991, 65–66).

Trish Mayo's picture of some figurines found at Harappa

The ancient debris discovered on the upper layers of Cemetery R-37 is itself an interesting archaeological find. As advanced as Harappa's drainage system was, its solid waste sanitation system was quite rudimentary and partially the reason for physical shifts in the population within the city over the history of its lifespan. The population of the city, elite and non-elite, simply piled their solid waste on the edge of the city, and when the waste got to be too much of a problem, the population would shift to another location.

For much of Harappa's history, the primary city dumps were located next to both cemeteries (Kenoyer 1991, 34), which can potentially tell researchers much about the city and its people. In all likelihood, the dumps were located there due to a combination of being convenient yet far enough from the housing. It is interesting, though, that the city's primary dumps would be located so close to the cemeteries, which perhaps indicates that the ancient Harappans' ideas of death and the afterlife were not as developed as in other ancient cultures, or that earthly and mundane considerations played a lesser role in one's successful entry into the afterlife.

Harappa's Culture

Harappa and Mohenjo-daro are believed to have been the two largest Indus Valley cities, and, in most ways, they are the best preserved. The baths and drainage systems paint a picture of a society that was as advanced as that of their contemporaries in Mesopotamia and Egypt, and the cemeteries show that they had somewhat developed ideas about the afterlife. The pottery and figurines discovered in Cemetery R-37 demonstrate that there was a craft industry at Harappa, but there is no evidence of any monumental statuary. No statues of kings or deities on the level of those of Egypt, or even Mesopotamia for that matter, have been found in the Indus Valley. The well-known "Priest-King Statue" from Mohenjo-daro is the best-known example of Indus statuary, but it is fragmentary and broken, and its identity as a king is not accepted by all scholars (Possehl 2002, 115).

Although there is an apparent absence of royal statuary, Harappa is where some of the best examples of Indus statuary have been found. Just south of the granary on Mound F, Vats discovered one of the more interesting examples of Indus statuary during the 1928–29 excavation season. The statue is a red jasper nude male statue, but only the torso is intact. Due to the stratum that the statue was excavated from, Vats dated it between 2200 and 1900 BCE, or the end of the Mature Harappan phase. The statue is about three-and-a-half inches tall (Possehl 2002, 111), so it may have measured about six inches when complete.

Another interesting small statue Vats discovered was about the same size as the jasper male but was made of gray stone. This piece was also discovered near the granary, so it is also thought to have come from the Mature Harappan phase, although that is not confirmed. Scholars believe that the statue was of a dancing girl, similar to others discovered at Mohenjo-daro (Possehl 2002, 112).

The lack of any large number of colossal statuary or statuary associated with monuments raises questions about the nature of Indus Valley society in general and at Harappa in particular. If there were absolute monarchs at Harappa or any of the other Indus Valley cities, then one would expect to find at least a few examples of statues of those rulers, as have been discovered in abundance in Egypt and Mesopotamia. The absence of such statues certainly does give some credence to the idea of a "stateless" society in Harappa. Since the Harappans did have access to stone and other materials for building colossal statuary, and since their contemporaries in Egypt and Mesopotamia built colossal statues of their rulers, historians don't understand why this society would not have done so, and thus question whether they had a similar structure of government. This is not to say that Harappan society was necessarily democratic, but that it possibly functioned under a system where there was less emphasis on an absolute ruler. That said, none of this alone is enough to make any definitive judgments on the nature of Harappan government.

As noted earlier, writing can be traced to the earliest phase of Harappan culture, and the earliest known symbols that were later used in writing were discovered at Harappa. These symbols represent what was probably the oldest Indus script, or a forerunner to it, and are dated from 2800-2600 BCE (Kenoyer 1999, 69). Overall, nearly 1,000 seals with writing have been discovered at Harappa, and nearly 70% of those were found on Mound F (Wright 1991, 82).

Besides having what appears to be a short sentence or a word or two, these seals were often inscribed with the image of an animal or mythical figure. The most common figure on the Harappan seals is a unicorn, and unicorn figurines were also discovered in different locations at Harappa (Kenoyer 1999, 87). Since the unicorn is a mythical creature, one logical assumption is that seals with unicorns, and possibly all or most seals, have a religious or theological context, although, like many aspects of Harappan society, it is impossible to say for sure. Other creatures and symbols found on seals with writing at Harappa include zebus (Possehl 2002, 112), humans (Possehl 2002, 145), and swastikas (Kenoyer 1999, 108).

One of the more interesting seals discovered at Harappa, and one that may someday tell scholars more about Indus religion, is the so-called "proto-Shiva" seal. The top of the seal has an inscription in the Indus language and below it sits what appears to be a human figure in a yogic position. It became known as "proto-Shiva" because the Harappan seal bears a strong similarity to the iconography of the Hindu god Shiva (Kenoyer 1999, 113). Not all scholars believe that the figure on the seal is a representation of Shiva, but others believe it is and point to it as an example of one element of Hinduism's Dravidian or at least pre-Aryan roots. Still other scholars believe that it is actually an argument for the Harappans being Aryans, instead of pre-Aryans as is generally believed (Bryant 2001, 162–4).

The large number of seals and artifacts with writing discovered at Harappa suggests that the city may have been an administrative and/or religious center. Based on examples from Egypt and Mesopotamia, the extant written texts at Harappa may also point toward it being a center of learning in the Indus Valley. Given that the ziggurats of Mesopotamia and the temples of Egypt functioned partially as scribal schools, the same may have been true at Harappa, and it's possible young men learned the craft of writing in one or more of the rooms in the granary.

Harappa's growth was steady through the Early and Mature Harappan phases, and since it did not suffer any widespread collapse between periods, the majority of the growth took place during the Mature Harappan phase as the city grew to as many as 50,000 people. The true growth was in the level of urban sophistication. Excavations of Mound F have revealed that during the early Mature Harappan phase there was a major shift in the production of finished goods both in the amount and type of production. Before this transition, production of goods primarily took place in private homes, which would obviously limit the type and amount of goods produced.

By the Mature Harappan phase, production approached a more industrial level, shifting to a larger area dedicated solely to industry. 14 houses were excavated on Mound F that are believed to be part of a "workmen's quarter," similar to Deir el-Medina in Egypt and other places in the ancient Near East (Wright 1991, 71).

Not surprisingly, the growth in industrial production at Harappa coincided with the city's growing international influence. As the civilization expanded, the Indus Valley had extensive trade connections with the kingdoms of Mesopotamia and was known in that region as Meluhha.

Besides the Akkadian texts that describe the trade, there have been plenty of artifacts recovered from Mesopotamia, central Asia, and the Persian Gulf region that attest to these contacts, including seals with Indus script from Ur, unicorn seals from Kish, and swastika seals found throughout the Near East (Possehl 2002, 222–6). Indus-style stamp seals, which are believed to have originated in Harappa, have also been found as far north as the site of Altyn Depe, which is in the modern state of Turkmenistan (Possehl 2002, 230). In turn, standardized weights, etched carnelian beads, and specific pottery types indicative of the Persian Gulf show that the Harappans imported goods and ideas as well (Wright 1991, 72).

The architectural discoveries made at Harappa can tell modern scholars much about life in the city. The walls, workshops, and some of the smaller finished products discovered in Harappa and abroad indicate that the city was very vibrant and probably driven by trade. Merchants from Mesopotamia, central Asia, and Persia would have been in the city at any given time, adding to its population and the mix of languages that no doubt would have been heard within its walls. The far-flung trade and many of the finished products recovered in Harappa also show that it was a wealthy city relative to other cities around the world at the time. The large number of objects with writing on them also demonstrates that at least a certain segment of Harappa was educated and literate. Harappa was also likely either a government or religious center, as evidenced by the so-called granary, where people from throughout the Indus Valley may have come for religious pilgrimages and possibly tax/tribute purposes.

However, all of this says more about the elite class in Harappa, not necessarily the vast majority of the population. The information does not provide concrete evidence about how Harappans lived on a day-to-day basis, and it doesn't indicate who the Harappans were ethnically or biologically. Thus, researchers continue trying to determine whether they were genetically related to any of their neighbors.

The remains of different animal bones have been discovered throughout Harappa, along with some plant remains, which has revealed much about the ancient Harappan diet. Whenever archaeologists discover animal bones at an ancient site, they have to determine if the bones were placed there after a religious ritual or due to food consumption. The context in which the animal bones were discovered at Harappa indicates they were consumed for food, which may or may not say something about the religion of the Indus Valley Civilization.

How much the animal remains say about religion at Harappa is difficult to determine, but it is easy to see what people ate at Harappa. Many of the animal bones were discovered on Mound E in the Mature Harappan strata, and among the most immediately recognizable were bovine bones. This is somewhat interesting considering that the Hindu religion forbids the consumption of cattle as it is a sacred animal, but the Harappans apparently had no such proscription. The remains of the cattle show they were a tall, light species that may have been specially bred at Harappa (Meadow 1991, 94).

Although cattle were certainly consumed at Harappa, sheep and goats were apparently more important. Both types of animals were domesticated in the early Neolithic Period at other sites in the Near East, so it is no surprise that their remains were found in abundance at Harappa. Sheep, though, were apparently more popular, with their bones being found at a nearly 4:1 ratio to goats (Meadow 1991, 97). There could be several reasons why sheep were the dominant animal at Harappa, but availability was probably not one of them. Similar to the cattle, the bones of the sheep and goats at Harappa show variation from those of other cities during the same periods, which indicates they were selectively bred, although unlike the cattle, Harappan sheep tended to be shorter and thicker (Meadow 1991, 96). Meadow believed that the evidence suggests that there is a strong likelihood that sheep were the primary focus of domestication and breeding at Harappa, and that they were used for clothing and fat as well as food (Meadow 1991, 102).

Archaeological evidence shows that fish was also an important part of the diet in Harappa, which is not surprising when given that the Indus River and its tributaries played a central role in the life of the civilization. Fish as a food source differs from the mammals discussed above because those animals were fully domesticated and presumably kept in pens or some other defined space. Fish, though, are never truly domesticated, even when they are kept in fish farms as they are today in some places, so they were "harvested" in the earlier periods of human history. Although nets are the most efficient way to capture large numbers of fish and are used today in south Asia, due to the nature of the material, none have been found extant at Harappa. A number of fishhooks have been found at Harappa though, and a scene from a pottery sherd recovered from Mound AB depicts men using what appear to be fishing nets (Belcher 1991, 117–8).

An analysis of fish bone fragments shows that there was quite a variety available to the people of Harappa. During the 1990 excavation season, archaeologists uncovered more than 1,500 fish fragments from 856 identified specimens, almost half of which were catfish (Belcher 1991, 113). The remains were found at Mound E and Mound AB, which indicates that the diet of the Harappans did not significantly change from the Mature Harappan to the Late Harappan periods. The larger fish would have been harvested locally or nearby, since meat from larger fish could not be adequately dried with the available techniques and technology at that time (Belcher 1991, 111).

Since Harappa was located some distance from the Indian Ocean, most of the recovered bone samples were of freshwater fish, but there were some marine catfish among the remains. These would have been smaller fish that were dried and salted before being transported up the Indus River to the Harappa region (Belcher 1991, 114). The existence of marine fish is another example of the thriving market of Harappa - as raw and finished materials left for the coast, dried fish was just one of the many commodities to make its way back to Harappa with either native or foreign merchants.

Other archaeological evidence indicates that the Harappans actually had quite balanced diets, and that in addition to the meats they consumed, they ate a number of plant foods. Archaeologists have been able to collect and catalog a number of different plant remains from Harappa, among the largest collection from the Indus Valley. Wheat, barley, and legumes were the major crops grown and consumed by the Harappans (Miller 1991, 121), and evidence shows that Harappans also collected some wild plants, such as the fruit jujube. They also collected wood for crafts and fuel.

Reeds were also collected to make matting and some types of boats, although it is not known if any of these collections were centrally organized (Miller 1991, 122). Historians assume that in the case of wood and reeds at least, some type of organized collection was done by the government, but that remains to be confirmed.

The constant flooding of the Indus River and its tributaries raises questions about Harappan farming techniques, but those too remain unanswered (Miller 1991, 122). Due to the nature of Indus Valley flooding and the seasonal monsoons, one would think that farming in the ancient Indus Valley probably resembled that of ancient Egypt, where the peasants scheduled their planting and harvesting around the annual flooding of the Nile River.

Human remains can also tell much about the way in which a people lived. For instance, although the human remains may only be bone fragments, teeth remains can provide clues about people's diets, and the condition of limb bones can reveal if the people were laborers or not. But more importantly as far as the Indus Valley Civilization is concerned, human remains may be able to tell scholars what ethnicity the Harappan people were. So many aspects of the Indus Valley Civilization remain a mystery, including what the people may have looked like and who they may have been related to genetically. If the language could be deciphered, it could potentially give scholars a solid place to begin in that respect, but even that would not necessarily offer definitive proof. It also would have helped if the Harappans depicted themselves in their art as the Egyptians, Hittites, Minoans, and people of ancient Mesopotamia did, but the images are few and far between.

Based on the figurines discovered at Harappa and Mohenjo-daro, Jan Fairservis created a drawing showing several different ancient Harappan men and women, of different types. Most are seen as darker Caucasians racially (Possehl 2002, 120–1). Many scholars believe that the ancient Harappans were Dravidians, similar to the people of southern India today, but that remains unproven. In fact, examinations of human remains from the cemeteries at Harappa may suggest otherwise. In the early 1990s, archaeologists examined the remains of 90 individuals taken from the Mature Harappan cemetery at Harappa, Cemetery R37C, and determined that most were young adults or middle age, with very few juveniles located there (Hemphill et. al. 1991, 139). The examination of the bones revealed some interesting facts that were somewhat surprising, and while the study did not allow for genetic testing, the archaeologists did compare, among other things, bone density and size of the Harappa samples with those from other parts of the Indus Valley and the Near East. The human remains from Harappa indicated affinities with those of the other peoples from the northern part of the Indus Valley, but they were actually different than those from Mohenjo-daro (Hemphill et. al. 1991, 172). The skeletal differences between the people of Harappa and Mohenjo-daro is interesting, but it can possibly be explained by a range of factors including diet and environment.

What is even more interesting, though, is that the Harappan remains also show an affinity with the people of the Near East (Hemphill et. al. 1991, 173). This revelation is not so mysterious when one considers the close trade connections between Harappa and the Near East. As goods were exchanged between Harappa and Mesopotamia, the Persian Gulf, and central Asia, it appears that people were also being exchanged.

Kalibangan's Early Years

The ancient site of Kalibangan is located in what is now known as the Ghaggar-Hakra Valley, just over 200 miles northwest of the modern city of Delhi in the region of Rajasthan (Avari 2007, 32). As mentioned earlier, Kalibangan was located on the banks of the Saraswati River, which is now a dry riverbed, but back then, the Saraswati River ran parallel with the Indus River in a primarily east-northeast direction from the Indian Ocean, through the plains of northcentral India into the Siwalik foothills of the Himalayan Mountain range (Kenoyer 1999, 28-29). Since the Indus Valley is a wide, flat valley, there were many tributaries of both the Indus and Saraswati rivers in antiquity.

The two major tributaries of the Saraswati River were the Sutlej River and Drishadvati River, and Kalibangan was located at the confluence of the Saraswati and Drishadvati, on the southern escarpment of the Saraswati River (Kenoyer 1999, 28). Recently, airborne electromagnetic surveys have revealed numerous paleochannels from the pre-Harappan and Harappan periods (Mishra and Mallick 2008, 1657), which indicate that even more tributaries once existed there, as well as artificially constructed canals. Kalibangan's location reveals much about its life and importance in the wider Harappan Civilization, including being situated on an escarpment, which was more than likely the result of defensive considerations.

The city's location relative to one major river and several tributaries suggests that trade played a role in its foundation, and it may also explain why the site flourished in the Early and Late Harappan Periods. Kalibangan would have served as a central point for trade coming from deeper in the Indus Valley to the coast and from foreign locations, such as Mesopotamia, headed into the interior. The fact that the Saraswati may not have reached the sea during the Early or Mature Harappan Periods (Possehl 2002, 9) means that overland routes were probably required for transporting goods between the river and the sea. There were existing overland routes that connected the Indus and Saraswati Rivers, which also would have placed Kalibangan in a prime location.

There is some evidence that Kalibangan's location was chosen for religious or spiritual reasons. The Indus and Saraswati Rivers had religious and practical significance for both the Harappans and the Aryans who came later. In fact, the Saraswati River may have been even more highly regarded by the Aryans. The presence of what appears to have been a Harrapan ritual structure just outside of Kalibangan, on the banks of the Saraswati River, would certainly suggest the river held religious significance for the Harrapan people.

Electromagnetic surveys of the area around Kalibangan and other archaeological discoveries show that it was once an agriculturally rich region. The canals would have been used to transport people between rivers, and also to irrigate the fields of the area. Rich alluvial soils from the Saraswati River provided the perfect ground to grow a wide array of different crops that were needed to sustain a relatively large and growing population. Evidence shows that the people of Kalibangan developed advanced agricultural techniques from an early point, and these were needed to feed the population of a relatively large and growing city.

Indus Valley cities varied widely in terms of physical size and population, ranging anywhere from what would be a small village of a couple dozen people to cities of 50,000 people or more. Modern archaeologists and Indianologists rank the Indus cities by size into three categories, or tiers. The first tier is comprised of cities that encompassed areas of 200 acres or more (Avari 2007, 43). Harappa and Mohenjo-daro were the two most prominent of the tier one cities, but there are about a half-dozen other cities that match the criteria of the category. Most of the cities in this category had populations of at least 10,000 people, while some, such as Harappa and Mohenjo-daro, had populations that were greater. Besides the size in area and population, all of the tier one cities also had walls and other permanent structures, such as baths.

The second tier of cities were slightly smaller than the first tier, with an average of 50 acres and populations ranging from the hundreds up to around 10,000 people. Although the tier two Indus cities were smaller than the tier one cities, they possessed many of the same architectural features, including walls and other buildings (Avari 2007, 44). Kalibangan was a tier two city, with an estimated population of at least 1,000 people, a wall, and other architectural features that were also present at Harappa and Mohenjo-daro. Kalibangan also had a few unique architectural features that will be discussed further below.

The process by which the Indus Valley region came to be settled was gradual, but once Kalibangan and the other cities were built, their development was relatively quick. Humans lived in the Indus Valley for quite some time during the Paleolithic and Neolithic Periods, first hunting and gathering their food, and then developing agriculture around 8000 BCE (Avari 2007, 27). The march toward civilization was similar to the processes in Egypt and Mesopotamia occurring around the same time, with small, semi-permanent settlements becoming permanently established and developing as focal points for trade, protection and regional power. The permanent settlements grew into towns and cities, regional economies developed, and specialized trades became important. The settlement at Kalibangan began around 3000 BCE and lasted until about 2600 BCE (Avari 2007, 32).

As with any archeological site from such an early period in human development, much of the material excavated from Early Harappan Kalibangan consists of pottery and pottery shards. Despite not being as impressive as other archaeological material, such as statues or large monuments, pottery is often just as important because it provides archaeologists with a lot of information about the people being examined, ranging from daily habits to their ethnicity. Pottery is often used by archaeologists to create a chronology of a society when written records are lacking or unable to be deciphered, as is the case for the Harappan Civilization.

Early Harappan pottery in Kalibangan has many similarities to pottery discovered at other sites around the Saraswati River, which led to Harappan scholars terming this early period of Harappan culture the period of "regionalization" (Dikshit 2012-2013, 3). In terms of the Harappan Civilization, the period of regionalization actually began before the Early Harappan Period and lasted for its entirety (Kenoyer 1999, 24). As the name indicates, it was marked by the importance of regional urban centers.

For a number of reasons, Kalibangan is believed to have been one of the primary centers along the Saraswati River during this time and the Mature Harappan Period. The fact that Kalibangan was one of the largest cities along the Saraswati River, especially within its immediate vicinity, points to its importance; but pottery evidence also reveals much about Kalibangan's significance.

B. K. Thapar, one of the primary archaeologists at Kalibangan, identified six different types of pottery from the site, termed "fabrics." The types were given letter designations (A, B, C, D, E and F) in order to track them better in other sites throughout the Indus Valley, and in the years since Thapar's work at Kalibangan in the 1960s, several of these fabric types have been found at other sites in the Indus Valley (Garge 2010). The fact that Kalibangan pottery was found at other Indus sites is important in itself, but even more so when considering how widely distributed the pottery was and the fact that it was the most common type of pottery found in many places (Garge 2010). The fact that non-Kalibangan pottery was rare in Kalibangan is also important. All of this demonstrates that Kalibangan was an important regional center in the Early Harappan Period and that it at least wielded some amount of economic influence over neighboring cities and villages.

The pottery discovered at Kalibangan from the Early Harappan Period was certainly important, and so too were the bricks from this period. Early Harappan Kalibangan was already a sophisticated city, complete with streets, a wall, and other buildings, but in order to build those things, the people needed to make bricks, which is in itself an advance in civilization because it required knowledge of kilns. The knowledge needed to make and operate kilns demonstrates a level of cultural sophistication that is only common in the late Neolithic for other societies. Bricks excavated at Kalibangan from the Early Harappan Period were smaller than they were in the Late Harappan Period (Dikshit 2012-2013, 3), which indicates that new knowledge was brought to the city between the two periods. Much the way changes in pottery are often indicative of new cultural influence, or even a new culture in a specific city or region, the appearance of new brickmaking techniques also indicates new cultural influences.

Although not as exciting as other aspects of archaeology, a further examination of the bricks and brickmaking techniques may help reveal more about the overall construction of Kalibangan, and excavations at Kalibangan have revealed that it was a fully functioning city with many architectural features during the Early Harappan Period. The Indus Valley cities in general were not known for large religious monuments or temples, but the larger sites all had baths and other washing areas. The baths in particular have garnered much academic interest - at Mohenjo-daro, the so-called "Great Bath" was centrally located in the city, which indicates that it was unlikely to have been a public bath and was probably ritualistic in nature. (Kenoyer 1999, 64). Early Kalibangan also had baths and washing areas, although they were not as large as the Great Bath at Mohenjo-daro, and the ruins of latrines, drains and washing areas have also been uncovered on the Early Harappan level.

The people of Kalibangan also practiced irrigation along the plain just outside of the city (Kenoyer 1999, 42). The ancient canals, discovered through the electromagnetic surveys mentioned earlier, brought water from the Saraswati River to the plain, which allowed Kalibangan to grow in size and population.

Evidence indicates that by 2800 BCE, Early Harappan Kalibangan was a regional center and in many ways a smaller version of Mohenjo-daro and Harappa. Beginning around that time, Kalibangan's city planners began building streets along a grid pattern similar to the larger Indus Valley cities (Kenoyer 1999, 52). The development of the streets continued until about 2600 BCE and facilitated Kalibangan's growth as a regional center. As more merchants and travelers came through Kalibangan on trips along the Saraswati River, an efficient street system was needed to keep the city orderly and clean. The increase of people in and around Kalibangan may also have brought more trouble, although there is little evidence of any major problems coming from the outside. As mentioned earlier, some scholars believe that the streets of Indus cities had a religious significance, which, if so, likely also would have been the case at Kalibangan.

The single feature from Early Harappan Kalibangan that may indicate threats existing outside the city is the presence of a wall. Walls were a standard feature in all of the first and second tier Harappan cities, no doubt to protect the inhabitants from outside forces, but there are other reasons why walls were built. Walls sometimes served to separate one class of people from another, such as nobles from lower classes, or to separate the sacred from the secular. Unfortunately, it is unclear why walls were built at Kalibangan, or at any other Harappan site, but either way, Kalibangan's Early Harappan wall was approximately 880 by 544 feet (a relatively large circuit for the era) and was built in two phases (Possehl 2002, 74). In the first phase, the wall was made of mudbrick and was about six feet thick. The second phase of construction on the wall thickened it to nearly 13 feet, with the face plastered in mud (Possehl 2002, 74). Such a large and thick wall would suggest that the leaders of Kalibangan feared an attack from the outside or perhaps were attacked at some point in their history, but there is scant archaeological evidence of any major attacks on the city, and there is no evidence of major military activity on the part of Kalibangan's residents. Until more evidence is uncovered, the existence of the Indus Valley Civilization's walls will remain a topic of speculation.

The end of Early Harappan Kalibangan was the result of a number of factors, as was the case for Early Harappan society in general, but one important factor was unique to the city of Kalibangan. The overextension of the economic and political networks certainly played a role, although they were probably not direct factors in Kalibangan's decline. The networks that became disrupted in the larger cities of Mohenjo-daro and Harappa would have affected Kalibangan by temporarily ending or limiting the connections that the sub-regions within the Indus Valley shared. Kalibangan certainly would have experienced a level of impoverishment and a loss of prestige, but the city continued on and retained some regional influence.

The desiccation of the rivers that adversely affected some of the Indus Valley cities at the end of the Early Harappan Period does not appear to have been much of a factor in Kalibangan's decline. Although the Saraswati River did dry up, it did not happen until hundreds of years later, at the end of the Mature Harappan Period (Haywood 2005, 77). With that said, the drying up of other rivers in the Indus Valley would have contributed to the overall impoverishment of the region through reduced agricultural input and trade. Excavations from the Early Harappan level at Kalibangan also show no evidence of a burn layer, which serves to rule out potential explanations rather than offering any (Possehl 2002, 49). The lack of a burn layer more than likely rules out an invasion - as invasions are usually accompanied by extensive burning - or a widespread natural fire. Other signs of destruction also tend to accompany burn layers, especially if they are the result of humans, which is not the case with Early Harappan Kalibangan. Burn layers and apparent human destruction are evident at other Early Harappan sites (Possehl 2002, 48), but, for whatever reason, Kalibangan avoided this fate.

It appears that Early Harappan Kalibangan declined alongside the general decline in the Indus Valley, but there is also evidence to show that the city did suffer a disaster. Excavators of Kalibangan detected an extreme displacement of strata at the Early Harappan level, which points toward a major event or disaster happening quickly. Since there is not an accompanying burn layer, archaeologists have concluded that the displacement was probably caused by an earthquake (Possehl 2002, 48). This earthquake does not appear to have affected many other cities in the Harappan Civilization (or it its effects were masked by human destruction), but since the apparent earthquake was big enough to cause the strata at the Early Harappan level to be displaced, the destruction was probably bad enough that it restricted growth at Kalibangan. That said, the city did not take long to rebuild, because by about 2500 BCE, Kalibangan was growing again as a part of the Mature Harappan Period.

Mature Harappan Kalibangan

Scholars once believed that the Early Harappan Period (previously known as the Pre-Harappan Period) and the Mature Harappan Period represented two related but distinct cultures, but as excavations conducted in the Indus Valley led to more understanding of the Harappan culture, it became clear that there was more continuity between the two periods than there were differences, so scholars began to see them as different developmental phases but not distinct cultures. Indeed, Kalibangan seems to have retained its Early Harappan attributes, but there were numerous additions made to the city and possible influences from an outside cultural group.

Among the changes was the city's growth in size. Archaeologists believe that the city grew in this phase to have at least 1,000 people, and possibly slightly more (Possehl 2002, 173). The walls prevented the city from sprawl and assisted modern archaeologists in coming to a conclusion regarding its size, along with the fact that they are able to compare the size of Kalibangan to the larger well-excavated sites of Harappa and Mohenjo-daro. Excavations of the Kalibangan cemetery (discussed further below) also help historians estimate an approximate size for the city, and while it may not seem like a very large city by today's standards, for the Bronze Age it was quite large and would have been full of life.

A visitor to Mature Harappan Kalibangan would have found a complete market along the perfectly laid out streets. A noble or member of the elite would have been visible as well, living on the highest point or citadel of the city (Avari 2007, 32). Citadels were common in many places in antiquity and were usually the site of the city's most sacred temple, as well as the residences of the elites. Citadels were also the most defensible part of the city and often the site of a last stand made by defenders.

Although it is not known for sure what the purpose of Kalibangan's citadel was, some reasonable conclusions have been made based on the available archaeological evidence. The citadel of Kalibangan was built over the Early Harappan phase of the town, and sometime around 2500 BCE, when the population of the town rapidly grew, the area just below the citadel began to be populated. Excavations of the site have determined that most of the city's population lived in the lower town (Possehl 2002, 76), and this population distribution of Mature Harappan Kalibangan would seem to suggest that the elites inhabited the citadel while the peasants, tradesmen and merchants lived in the lower city. The markets would have been located in the lower city, and any foreign merchants visiting the city would also have stayed in the lower city. The elites would have been better protected in the citadel in the event of an attack, and the view would have afforded them a strategic view of the area. There is also other archaeological evidence that suggests Kalibangan's citadel was home to the city's elites.

Although no monumental temple was uncovered at Kalibangan and there are scant examples of such architecture even in the largest Indus cities, the citadel of Kalibangan shows some signs of religious activity and significance. A number of platforms have been uncovered that may have served as altars, along with the ruins of baths nearby that possibly had a sacred context. A number of mudbrick platforms were uncovered on the southern half of the citadel. These structures, which have been termed "fire altars" by a number of scholars, were carefully built oval structures that were sunk in the ground and lined with mud plaster or bricks (Possehl 2002, 76). The sacred aspects of fire in the later Aryan culture and its possible connection to Kalibangan will be discussed further below, but for now it is important to consider that the altars were discovered in both public and residential areas of the citadel (Bryant 2001, 160). The fact that the altars were public would certainly point toward a religious activity shared by the community, and the fact that some were in private residences does not necessarily mitigate this idea. After all, private religious practice has been documented alongside state religion in the Bronze Age cultures of Egypt and Mesopotamia. In ancient Egypt, for instance, private practice of religion was commonly done by individuals donating votive stelae and statues to temples.

Although there is no evidence of similar practices in the ancient Indus Valley, ritual bathing may have been akin to this practice. A well and baths are located next to the fire altars, and this layout was common at many Indus sites. The location of the baths next to the fire altars on the Kalibangan citadel appears to have religious significance, possibly indicating a ritual cleansing area that one must go through before tending to the fires. Also located next to the baths was a bovine burial pit, immediately leading to more academic discussion and debate because cows became a sacred animal later in Indian religion. Those who believed that the Aryans were native to India and possibly related to the Harappan Civilization, drawing from knowledge about Vedic Indian religion, have argued that the entire context of the fire altars, baths, and bovine burial must have been sacred in nature (Bryant 2001). While most historians do not agree with the native Aryan theory, many are willing to accept that the mudbrick platforms discovered at Kalibangan were religious in nature and that the area of the south citadel was a sacred space. With that said, others believe that the fire altars were actually baking pits and that the purpose of the area was much more mundane (Bryant 2001, 161).

Both the citadel and the lower city of Mature Harappan Kalibangan had walls. The existing Early Harappan walls around the upper city were retained, and a new wall was built for the new, lower city. There were three gate entrances to the upper city and two to the lower city. Mudbrick homes were in both parts of the city, although none were located on the southern part of the citadel, further suggesting that was probably where a sacred area was located (Possehl 2002, 77). The streets of the lower town generally ran in a north-south direction, terminating at the walls.

A structure was also excavated just east of the lower town, and although its purpose remains uncertain, it is strongly believed to have had a ritual significance (Possehl 2002, 77). The probable ritual structure overlooked the Saraswati River, which was a sacred site for the ancient Harappans, and the site of this supposed ritual structure may be a reason why Kalibangan was built where it was, but further work will need to be conducted before anything can be confirmed. Unfortunately, much of how the people of Kalibangan practiced their religion, or even what their religion was, remains conjecture at this point.

Almost 1,000 feet west-southwest of the citadel are the remains of the Kalibangan cemetery. The cemetery is located downwind from the settlement and downstream from the floodplain (Possehl 2002, 171), which demonstrates a certain degree of practical planning by the original builders. The rich alluvial fields near Kalibangan would have been untainted by the decay of human bodies, and any seepage from the bodies into the water supply would have been minimal or even nonexistent. The location may also have had a religious significance since corpses were viewed as impure by many of the peoples of ancient India. This belief was articulated clearly in later periods of Indian history, as well as in Iran in the *Avesta*, and it also applied to the Harappans.

The cemetery was discovered rather accidentally after a heavy rainfall produced outlines in the soil that suggested burials or graves, and the excavation of the cemetery revealed 102 inhumation sites, which is too small to represent the entire city of Kalibangan over its long history (Possehl 2002, 173). The number suggests that the cemetery was used primarily or exclusively by the elites of Kalibangan, but a closer examination uncovered even more complexities in the necropolis.

As archaeologists began their work at the Kalibangan cemetery, they quickly realized that it was no ordinary necropolis. In fact, they only found human remains in 88 of the 102 graves, and after further examination, the graves with no human remains were classified into two types, which were actually cenotaphs (Possehl 2002, 173). Traditionally speaking, a cenotaph is a type of tomb where the body has been stored elsewhere. The owner's body may never have been in the cenotaph, or it was for awhile and reinterred somewhere else. Whatever the reason for the lack of a body, the tomb remains as a monument for the owner. In the ancient world they were common for elites, and at Kalibangan there may have been multiple reasons for their existence.

The cenotaphs contained pottery and other possessions that would have had some value, obviously pointing toward a belief in the afterlife. It also indicates that the graves were intended to be more functionally for the dead than for the living. Other than the items that were found in the graves, there is no evidence that the living brought offerings or other gifts to the cenotaphs once they were covered.

More importantly, though, the cenotaphs were located in a different section of the cemetery than the graves containing human remains (Possehl 2002, 173). This difference in burial type and location suggests a few different possibilities that could reveal more about life at Kalibangan. For example, the separate locations of the cenotaphs and the normal graves indicates that the two groups represented different social classes, although archaeologists are currently unable to determine which, if either, of the groups was the elite. Another possibility is that the cenotaph graves belonged to individuals who died away from Kalibangan – perhaps on a military campaign, a diplomatic mission, or, more likely, conducting long-distance trade – and members of their families were unable to retrieve their bodies (Possehl 2002, 173). It is even possible that the spatial separation of the different grave sites and the manner of burial could also indicate more than one ethnic group inhabiting Kalibangan (Possehl 2002, 174).

It could be the case that since the number of graves is much lower than the actual population of Kalibangan, the graves were all for members of the elite, but there were two different groups of elites, such as nobles and priests or soldiers.

A picture of the passage to the cemetery

All of these possibilities are plausible and not necessarily exclusive of one another. India has always been a land of many different ethnic groups, so such theories represent a highly realistic possibility. It is also possible that the elites were of a different ethnic group than the majority of the people of Kalibangan, and since the elite would have traveled more, it is reasonable to postulate that they may have died while on diplomatic missions away from the city.

Agriculture was the lifeblood of all pre-modern civilizations, and especially for urbanized societies such as the Mature Harappan Civilization. Mature Harappan Kalibangan may have been alive with trade and markets and presided over by an elite class residing on the citadel, but their sustenance came from the surrounding area. Farming techniques and the food produced in the fields would have been much like they are today in that region of modern India. The farmers would have been reliant on the seasonal rains and monsoons to determine planting and harvesting times, and they would have used oxen and manpower to work the fields. The vast majority of the population would have survived on a diet heavy in wheat, barley, and rice, with occasional vegetables and meats thrown in for taste and variety. The elites living on Kalibangan's citadel, though, would have had the luxury of an expanded menu due to their control of trade (Kenoyer 1999, 170).

Archaeological work at Kalibangan has revealed an abundance of evidence relating to agriculture. One of the most interesting discoveries was of a plowed Mature Harappan field just outside the town. Although this discovery may not sound like much, it is the earliest known plowed field in the world (Kenoyer 1999, 163). Domestic crop agriculture was being practiced in Egypt and Mesopotamia at the same time, but there is no evidence that those peoples ever plowed their fields. The plowed field of Kalibangan was most likely done by oxen, which were common animals in the region during the Mature Harappan Period (Kenoyer 1999, 163). The crops that were harvested in the first plowed field would have varied according to the season, but more than likely there would always have been something growing.

Agricultural production during this phase was localized. Cities located closer to the coast were more dependent on the monsoon for the growing season. The farmers in the monsoon-dominated region planted their crops in the summer, during or after the monsoon, and harvested them in the fall. Rice was one of the most common monsoon crops in the region of Gujarat by 2600 BCE, but it was grown later in the Indus Valley, including around Kalibangan (Kenoyer 1999, 163).

Since Kalibangan was located on the alluvial plain, its farmers followed a different planting and growing pattern and originally grew different crops. The fields of Kalibangan were planted in the fall, fed by winter rains, and harvested in the spring. Wheat and barley were the dominant crops in the alluvial region around Kalibangan, and besides the crops, agriculture around Kalibangan involved a variety of different animals, both for food and for work.

Extant seals from Kalibangan and other Indus cities can help historians deduce how animal husbandry was practiced in Mature Harappan Kalibangan. The prominence of bovine species on the seals, combined with modern farming practices, indicates that oxen played a prominent role as draft animals, and possibly as food as well (Kenoyer 1999, 162). Other animals that were consumed in sites throughout the Indus Valley include sheep, goats, and chickens (Possehl 2002,

83). Although the cow became a sacred animal later in Indian religion and consumption of them was proscribed, there is no evidence to suggest that the Harappans had similar religious sentiments.

Among the remains of animals that have been found at Kalibangan, none are more puzzling than those of equids. A terracotta figurine of a horse from the Indus site of Pirak has been dated to around 1600 BCE, which would place it at the end of the Harappan Civilization and in the Late Harappan Period (Kenoyer 1999, 177). This may not seem like a very important item, but it is generally believed that the Aryans first brought horses to India around that time or just after it.

The chronological overlap could explain the existence of that figurine, but not others that came earlier, or the remains of multiple horses found at Kalibangan. Equid bones, teeth, and figurines have all been discovered at Kalibangan, which raises many problems concerning Indian chronology, particularly regarding the later Aryan incursion. Some native Indian scholars believe that the equid evidence from Kalibangan indicates that the Aryans may have originated in India and lived simultaneously with the Harappans, or that the Aryans were even Harappans themselves. In contrast, other scholars simply argue that the equid remains at Kalibangan are not strong enough evidence from which to make sweeping chronological generalizations, and that the remains are consistent with strata from a later period when the Aryans had already introduced the horse to the region (Bryant 2001, 173). This may seem like a logical answer, but the drying of the Saraswati River and the depopulation of Kalibangan is generally believed to have taken place before the arrival of the Aryans in the region.

Kalibangan's decline was slow and gradual. Likely starting around 2000 BCE, the city was mostly depopulated and well on its way to being nothing but ruins by 1500 BCE. It was once believed that the warlike Aryans destroyed the Harappan Civilization, but that theory has completely fallen out of academic favor due to the lack of evidence demonstrating any kind of invasion. Today, most scholars believe that a combination of factors brought down the Harappan Civilization, and at Kalibangan specifically, environmental changes played a major factor. Thus, by the time the Aryans arrived in the region around Kalibangan, the Saraswati River was a shadow of its former self and Kalibangan was no longer a true city.

The overextension of trade and political networks was discussed earlier as one of the factors for the collapse of the overall Harappan Civilization, and this no doubt played a role in Kalibangan's decline. After 1800 BCE, there is no evidence of long-distance contact and trade between the Indus Valley and Mesopotamia, which was probably caused by a number of internal factors. Once trade networks were disrupted in the larger cities of Mohenjo-daro and Harappa, regional centers such as Kalibangan would also have been adversely affected (Kenoyer 1999, 173).

That said, the disruption to the trade networks alone would not have been enough to destroy Kalibangan, as evidenced by a transition to localization by some of the surviving Harappan cities from about 1900 BCE until 1300 BCE (Kenoyer 1999, 174). The region best suited to survive the decline and transition into the localization period was the coastal area, which was more immune to the capricious nature of the climate and the shifting of the rivers.

Recent studies suggest that the final nail in Kalibangan's coffin was a combination of changes in the Indus River and climate change. The concept of climate change has been politically charged in recent years, but even a cursory study of pre-modern history shows that slight changes in global climate patterns often had disastrous consequences for cities, kingdoms, and civilizations. In Kalibangan's case, the first of its problems came when sedimentation and tectonic movement pushed much of the water from the Saraswati River west into the Sutlej River. The Sutlej River in turn sent that water into the Indus River, then east into the Yamuna River, which flowed into the Ganges system (Kenoyer 1999, 173). The changing river patterns caused flooding along the Indus, which led to refugees and other problems in the biggest cities. Secondly, and more important for Kalibangan's immediate survival, it sped up the process of the Saraswati River's desiccation.

Stratigraphic evidence shows that along with the changing river patterns, a prolonged period of decreasing rainfall contributed to accelerating the drying up of the Saraswati River. The area around Kalibangan experienced significant rainfall beginning around 3000 BCE, which coincided with its rise to regional prominence at the beginning of the Early Harappan Period. By the early Mature Harappan Period, that rainfall had peaked, but by 1000 BCE it had decreased tremendously from where it had been 2,000 years prior (Dikshit 2012-2013).

Once the Saraswati River had dried up or nearly dried up, it was just a matter of time before Kalibangan was abandoned. The river provided one of the primary sources of transportation for trade, as well as irrigation for the fields. With no source of water or food, the people simply left.

It seems that Kalibangan's death was rather anti-climactic; but some historians still continue to search for evidence that invaders played a role in the city's demise. The first to articulate the Aryan invasion theory was Mortimer Wheeler, who in 1946 largely based his idea on passages from the *Rig Veda*. Scholars now know that not only was the *Rig Veda* compiled hundreds of years after the collapse of the Harappan culture, but that its use as a historical source is dubious at best (Possehl 2002, 238). Others have pointed to the sudden introduction of new pottery styles at some Indus sites and the discovery of unburied skeletons at Mohenjo-daro as evidence of invasion, but neither of these are proof that an invasion occurred (Kenoyer 1999, 174).

For many native Indian historians, the narrative has shifted to one where the Aryans were not invaders from outside of India, but native Indians who lived alongside and influenced Harappan culture. They point to Kalibangan as proof of their theory, arguing that the fire altars and the equid remains show a clear Aryan influence, long before they were believed to have entered India (Bryant 2001, 160). Where Wheeler once used the *Rig Veda* to argue that the Aryans destroyed the Harappan culture, native Indian scholars now use it to argue their alternate thesis.

Although Kalibangan ceased to be a settlement before the Aryans became the dominant people in northern India, its general vicinity and the Saraswati River in particular are mentioned in the *Rig Veda*. Most historians admit that some features of Harappan Civilization can be seen in the *Rig Veda*, but they also believe that the cities of the region, including Kalibangan, were clearly pre-Vedic (Avari 2007, 40).

Since the *Rig Veda* was first composed orally as early as 1700 BCE, some elements of Harappan society were still in existence and could thus be observed by the Aryans, but the references that relate to the Saraswati River are important to consider in terms of Kalibangan's lifespan. The Vedic texts refer to the region of Punjab/Indus Valley as Sapta-Sindhava, which is the "Land of the Seven Rivers" (Avari 2007, 1). The Saraswati River was clearly one of the seven rivers, and the Aryan goddess of learning was later associated with the river, which means that it was still viable when the Aryans arrived sometime after 1700 BCE.

In one verse, Saraswati is described as a life-giving embryo:

> "Let Vishnu prepare the womb; let Tvastr shape the forms. Let Prajapati shed the seed; let Dhatr place the embryo in you.

> "Place the embryo, Sinivali; place the embryo, Sarasvati. Let the twin Ashvins, the lotus-garlanded gods, place the embryo in you."

The Saraswati is often referred to in this anthropomorphic form, which could suggest that its existence as a river may have been over well before the oral Vedic verses were compiled. Other verses mention the life-giving abilities of the Saraswati River, including this one: "Your inexhaustible breast, Sarasvati, that flows with the food of life, that you use to nourish all that one could wish for, freely giving treasure and wealth and beautiful gifts – bring that here for us to suck."

Proponents of the native Aryan theory argue that this text proves that Aryans were native to India or at least lived there during the Harappan Civilization because the Saraswati River was still flowing. Based on his archaeological work at Kalibangan, B.B. Lal has argued that the Saraswati River was dried up at Kalibangan by 2000 BCE, which would put the Vedic references at an earlier date (Bryant 2001, 167-8).

The Layout of Mohenjo-daro

Mohenjo-daro was the largest city of the Indus Civilization from approximately 2600-1900/1800 BCE. The city was located in the core of the Indus dominion, between Harappa to the north and Dholvaria to the south, with the Baluchistan hills to the west and the Sarasvati River Valley to the east. Over 240 hectares large at its height, the city may have accommodated a population of anything between 35,000 to more than 100,000 people – an extraordinarily high number for cities in the world that time.[1]

There is no evidence of what – if anything – preceded the occupation of the site when the city was formed in the early third millennium BCE. The lack of any earlier settlement may be attributed to the annual floods of the Indus River – the tall platforms upon which Mohenjo-daro and other cities were built could not be assembled before Indus society was able to manage the required labor force and materials.[2] Using bore holes – a method by which deep holes are cut into the ground and its contents are examined for potential stratigraphy and depths of cultural layers – archaeologists have discovered that Mohenjo-daro has extraordinarily deep layers of cultural accumulation going to a deepness of between 7-15 meters.[3]

However, the deepest and earliest layers of the city have never been excavated. As such, the city's sudden genesis is shrouded in mystery. In a period of around 80 years the enormous artificial platforms were constructed, the drainage network assembled, the street system laid out, and most of the buildings erected. This metropolis was about one and a half times larger than Harappa, making it the largest settlement of the Indus Civilization found so far. The speed and size of this construction could only have been undertaken by some centralized administrative group involved in the collection and management of the required labor and materials.

Mohenjo-daro was divided into two general areas along a roughly northwest-southeast axis, in terms of architecture, function, and apparent levels of social segregation.[4] To the south and east is the so-called "lower city", while north and west is an artificial raised mound known as the "upper city" or "citadel", which contained the most monumental structures and prestigious dwellings of the settlement. A deep depression in between the two may have served as a major through road, though the material remains of this area have been obscured by centuries of floods from the Indus River. The entire city is around a thousand meters long north to south, and between 500-700 meters wide east to west. However, the latest archaeological surveys have revealed that an extensive suburban landscape spread from the southern and eastern limits of the citadel and lower city – and a lesser extent to the north – where vast suburban districts were buried without a trace beneath the alluvial plain for centuries.[5] The surveys also revealed a significant lack of urban extension made to the west of the high artificial platform. An unknown number of buildings existed in this suburban landscape, but the number was likely in the hundreds if not thousands.

The artificial platforms and the exterior and interior of almost all of the buildings at Mohenjo-daro were composed of mud brick walls built on top of a solid and long-lasting foundation of baked bricks. Bricks made of baked, unbaked, and sun-dried mud endure for, at most, a few

---

[1] Jansen, 1993

[2] Jansen, M. (2002) "Settlement Networks of the Indus Civilization." In S. Settar and Ravi Korisettar (eds) *Indian Archaeology in Retrospect. II. Protohistory. Archaeology of the Harappan Civilization.* New Delhi: Manohar. 105–126.

[3] McIntosh, 2008

[4] Vidale, M. (2010) "Aspects of Palace Life at Mohenjo-daro." *South Asian Studies*, 26:1. 59-76

[5] McIntosh, 2008

decades before collapsing under the effects of floods, heavy rains, occasional fires, earthquakes, and other shocks. These buildings thus required frequent maintenance, and often they were simply leveled and had a new structure built atop the previous foundations. To manufacture enough mass-produced bricks for a city of this scale would have required vast amounts of fuel, materials, and labor.

Moreover, other diverse kinds of materials had to be used in the construction of the city. There are a few buildings that make use of stone and wood.[6] Indeed, there is evidence suggesting that some of the largest buildings in the metropolis were made entirely of wood, which has left almost no trace today.[7] The residential buildings in the lower cities may have had wooden verandas, screens, staircases, and entire upper stories made of wood.[8] The mud brick walls would have once been covered in plaster. Asphalt and bitumen acquired from the Baluchistan hills were also frequently used in the city's hydraulic network.

A cycle of collapse and renewal must have been a regular occurrence in the lives of those living in Mohenjo-daro. Successive falls and restoration may have become part of the elite psyche, as future generations were encouraged to restore structures that had social and cultural importance. Due to this phenomenon, the layout of the city remained almost unchanged for its entire period of occupation, with the same street network and houses built upon the foundations of those that existed before – though deviations would often be made to the interior division of space, with walls and courtyards forming and disappearing at different times.

The citadel was an artificial platform made of sand and soil, and faced with a six meter thick wall of mud bricks held together with mud. It was extended and heightened at various points during the city's occupation, and today is roughly in the shape of a parallelogram rising to a height of between six and eighteen meters. However, the lowest layers of the mound have not yet been excavated, and underground layers might show that it was once even higher. Most of the features that are visible on the citadel date from the so-called Mature Harappan Period (approximately 2600 to 2500 BCE).

---

[6] Vidale, 2010
[7] Kenoyer, 2000
[8] Mackay, E. (1938) *Further Excavations at Mohenjo-daro.* New Delhi: Government of India

An early picture of the citadel

The presence of walls, fortified gates, and towers provide the citadel with its name, though no evidence has been found suggesting that these were ever used during conflict. No evidence of military conflict has been conclusively associated with the site, and few weapons were ever made in the city – though the presence of a barracks in the lower town has been suggested.[9] Indeed, most of the defenses were targeted towards natural threats, in particular the annual floods of the Indus. Many of the fortifications are clustered around the south-eastern corner of the acropolis. There are towers made of brunt brick and reinforced with massive wooden timbers, which guard a postern gate flanked by rectangular bastions – later replaced by a platform and a raised walkway with parapet.

---

[9] Wheeler, 1953

A picture of some of the city walls

On the southwestern corner is another brick and timber tower, which oversees the "granary" building. Also known simply as "the warehouse", this massive building shared a similar architectural style to the fortified towers, insofar as it combined brickwork with the use of solid wooden timbers. It consists of twenty seven blocks made of mud brick, reaching a height of almost two meters and occupying a total floor space of approximately nine thousand square feet. Each stone block had a vertical access point accessed by a narrow passageway, which would have been used to deposit and withdraw grain from the hollow blocks and also as ventilation to keep the stores of grain dry and prevent mold.

To the south of the "granary" is a grand staircase over seven meters wide leading to the acropolis from the level of the river plains. At the top of this staircase is a small bathroom structure, which one must pass before accessing the northern half of the citadel. A number of monumental structures were built in this area of the mound, each constructed upon an additional platform of their own. Of these, two in particular are quite extraordinary: the Great Bath and the College Square.

Saqib Qayyum's picture of the "Great Bath" on the citadel (with the Buddhist stupa in the background)

M. Imran's picture of the Great Bath

   The Great Bath is located a little distance west of the second century CE Buddhist stupa, which itself is located at the highest part of the citadel. The Great Bath is an enormous multistoried structure, 11 meters by 7 meters, containing a paved courtyard and basin around three meters deep. Flights of brick steps topped with wooden planks set into bitumen lead into the rectangular bath. Made of tightly set bricks, the basin was made completely watertight by a mortar made of gypsum and sealed with bitumen. Water was drained through an elaborate outlet, decorated with a curved corbelled arch, which led through a system of pipes before being discharged along the western edge of the citadel mound. The building also contained a small block of eight bathrooms, each "cubicle" unusually containing a small staircase leading to an upper space, the function of which is unknown. Water should not be solely attributed to its hygienic and cleaning functions; the more numinous qualities of water and cleanliness should be considered when interpreting what this building was used for. The complexity of this floor layout suggests that measures were taken to segregate their users. These rooms may have been used for ablutions – ceremonial cleansing – as part of a religious ritual whose practitioners desired a high degree of privacy and serenity.

The canal for the Great Bath

Nearby is the College Square, so called by early archaeologists at the site who believed it to have been used as a college for priests, though later interpretations argue that it might have been used as an elite residence.[10] This long building is 70 meters by 28 meters, and it features a square open courtyard 10 meters long on each side, surrounded on three sides by verandas that are reminiscent of monastic cloisters. The building has a complicated biography, with deep stratigraphy showing evidence of numerous changes made to the ground plan over the centuries of its occupation.

---

[10] Vidale, 2010

A picture of part of the surviving structures at the site

The lower city was also built on an artificial mound of sand and silt, to a height of about eight meters, and retained by a surrounding mud brick wall. It features the characteristic infrastructure of roads of the Indus Civilization: a right angled grid plan of streets. The lack of organic qualities to the street network that might suggest long-term growth indicates that it would have been laid out quite quickly by experienced town-planners.

There appear to have been two major thoroughfares crossing east-west through the lower city, each around ten meters wide. Broad streets extended to the north and south of the main roads, and a great number of lanes and alleys crossed east-west around the entire city. These streets were all unpaved, apart from the two main streets, which were covered in a layer of ceramic and broken bricks.[11]

More than 300 vernacular houses, workshops, and commercial buildings densely filled in the resulting city blocks. These were tall mud brick structures, with evidence of buildings that were two and even three stories tall. Many other buildings were only one story high but contained sprawling courtyards. Although of different sizes with such extensions, they were still markedly homogeneous in form. Entrance to most of the buildings was almost always via the narrow east-

---

[11] Jansen, 1993

west lanes, and there was a lack of windows on the lower floors throughout the city – perhaps as a security measure, or to maintain the structural integrity of the walls. These buildings would have been quite clean environments, consisting of floors paved with baked mud bricks, an effective drainage system, and efficient insulation provided by the thick mud brick walls.[12]

There were few very large buildings in the lower city. The eastern and south-eastern districts of the lower city were almost entirely occupied by workshops, which also appear to have been amongst the earliest buildings constructed on the site. Of particular note is the so-called "Little Bath". This mud brick building is surrounded by four pillars made of baked bricks, and the interior features a concentric layout of rooms surrounding a central well, with a large drain. The ground plan within seems to carefully imitate the Great Bath at a smaller scale. It might therefore have also emulated the ritualistic practices and numinous associations of the Great Bath.[13]

For most of the 20th and 21st centuries there was a notable lack of buildings that were definitively interpreted as temples or elite residences in the lower or upper city.[14] By extension, it was believed that the city was ruled by neither a king nor other wealthy individual or group.[15] Recently, some have argued that Mohenjo-daro's elite residences were clustered in the western and north-western areas of the city. The architectural complex atop the citadel mound may actually have been used as a palace – a large urban residence of an elite group – due to the monumental scale of the buildings and entrances and materials used in their construction. Some of the structures made use of extremely rare and expensive resources, as demonstrated by the massive ring-stone columns made of yellow banded limestone from Khadir, of Rajasthani Jaisalmer stone, or of cherty limestone from Rohri that might even have been painted red.[16]

Daily Life in Mohenjo-daro

Subsistence in the region was divided into two different forms of agriculture. Much like the present day, *rabi* ("winter") agriculture was the main form of cultivation practiced by the population of Mohenjo-daro's hinterland.[17] The Indus River was vital to farming, as the lush and fertile land on either side of the river was ideal for agriculture and pastoral farming during the winter months.

However, the Indus was prone to violent, unpredictable floods that spilled over its banks. This more often washed away fields rather than replenished them. The cycle of floods and rains, and planting and harvest, thus prevented a framework that governed life beside the river.

---

[12] Wilkins, H. (2005) "From Massive to Flimsy: The Declining Structural Fabric at Mohenjo-daro". In U. FrankeVogt and H.-J. Weisshaar (eds) *South Asian Archaeology*. Aachen: Linden Soft.136–46
[13] Vidale, 2010
[14] Mackay, 1938
[15] Possehl, 2002
[16] Vidale, 2010
[17] McIntosh, 2008

Grain was the most valuable commodity available to the city. Wheat and barley were the main crops grown, though some varieties of rye and pulses were also cultivated, unlike the southern Ganges river valley, where *kharif* (summer) farming can facilitate the production of rice and millet crops. Some summer crops that may have been cultivated around Mohenjo-daro include cotton and sesame. Cotton threads have been discovered at the city, representing the earliest evidence of cotton textiles ever found in the world.[18]

The Baluchistan hills were not suitable for agriculture, apart from sparse alluvial soils in isolated river valleys. Instead, the hilly, upland regions were used as pasturage for domesticated animals including sheep, goats, and cattle. Throughout the Indus period pastoral farmers residing in small-scale villages would live itinerant lifestyles, bringing their herds into the hilly uplands during the summer months, and moving back into the Indus River lowlands when winter came. Their upland settlements were established on small artificial mounds, such as those of the so-called Quetta culture.[19]

Some meat was also acquired through hunting game and by fishing. Forests of acacia, tamarisk, and euphorbia were found in the local highlands and lowlands of the Himalayas. These were home a range of wild game for hunting, and for gathering honey and edible plants such as juniper, jujube, almond, and pistachio.[20] Accurate depictions of tigers, buffalo, rhinoceros and elephants have all been identified on the seals made by Indus valley artisans, indicating that such animals were present in the in the region.

The Indus River Valley and surrounding regions were filled with useful resources used by the Harappan civilization. Metal ores, precious stones, asphalt and bitumen were excavated from deposits on the hills along the border of the Iranian plateau and nearby Rajasthan. These include salt, steatite, agate, carnelian, alabaster, copper, tin and others. Flint was mined in the Rohri Hills in Sindh, bitumen from the north-western areas of the Punjab, and precious gems were gathered from Kashmir.[21] Even gold could be panned from the fast-flowing upper courses of the Indus.

The residents of the upland villages would likely have traded these resources at the markets of Mohenjo-daro. Mud was above all the most invaluable resource available in the city, and would have been gathered from the banks of the Indus and sent to industrial districts of the city or suburban area to be fired or sun baked.

There was a general lack of monumental art, and the workshops of the city appear to have focused on making smaller objects. However, they made use of a wide variety of materials and innovative techniques in their crafts. Steatite – also known as soapstone – was used in abundance

---

[18] McIntosh, 2088
[19] Wheeler, 1953
[20] McIntosh, 2008
[21] *ibid*

to make jewelry and seals. Some steatite objects were glazed in the same process that eventually led to the creation of faience. One particularly fine steatite sculpture, of which only the torso remains, is known as the "Priest King" for its association with early claims that the Indus Civilization was a theocracy.[22] Innumerable steatite seals have also been discovered by archaeologists. Many depict human figures and animals, in addition to symbols and characters which are believed to be the Indus writing system. The precise use of these seals is unknown, though the most widely-held interpretation is that they were used in merchant transactions to identify ownership of precious goods.[23]

The *Shiva Pashupati* seal

---

[22] Wheeler, 1953

[23] Ratnagar, S. (2004) *Trading Encounters: From the Euphrates to the Indus in the Bronze Age.* New Delhi: Oxford University Press.

In addition to the mud brick industry, clay gathered from the banks of the Indus was used to create a number of terra cotta human and animal statuettes.[24] The close examination of these figures has led scholars to argue that the Indus people did not make the same distinctions between male and female as existed during the Common Era.[25] Other ceramics were acquired through trade with the hill villages. Beyond the city, the artifactual styles of the Indus Valley from approximately 2500 BCE display a remarkable level of standardization – apart from the diverse iconographic styles and characteristics found in the upland regions such as the stoneware ceramics bearing distinctive designs of elongated animals with large eyes, dots and circles, and floral motifs of the Kulli-Mehi culture, executed in black and red.[26]

---

[24] Ardeleanu-Jansen, A. (2002) "The Terracotta Figurines from Mohenjo-daro: Considerations on Tradition, Craft and Ideology in the Harappan Civilization (c. 2400-1800 BC)". In S. Settar and R. Korisettar (eds) *Indian Archaeology in Retrospect, Vol 2, Protohistory: Archaeology of the Harappan Civilization.* New Delhi: Manohar. 205-222.

[25] Clark, S. R. (2003) "Representing the Indus Body: Sex, Gender, Sexuality, and the Anthropomorphic Terracotta Figurines from Harappa". *Asian Perspectives* 42:2. 304-328.

[26] Wheeler, 1953

62

63

64

Pictures of male, female, and animal figurines

Other objects found in Mohenjo-daro include stone bangles, faience bead jewelry, textiles woven from cotton, wool, or goat hair, leather goods, and exquisite statuettes made of shell and copper. An early metalworking industry existed in the city. They primarily worked with copper, producing tools and inscribed tablets, though small objects of silver and gold were also made. The so-called "Dancing Girl" is a bronze statue discovered at Mohenjo-daro in the 1920s, and tentatively associated with the later periods of occupation at the site.

65

Joe Ravi's picture of "The Dancing Girl"

While many of these goods were produced in the industrial districts of the city, and the workshops that might have been present in the surrounding suburban landscape, Mohenjo-daro was also located at the center of an extensive trade network that provided access to rare and expensive commodities. The city served as a hub of commercial activity. A standardized system of weights is indicated by archaeological remains, and there may have been a caravanserai in the lower city – a roadside inn where merchants could store their cargo and rest overnight when they traveled through the region. The city was ideally situated to take advantage of trade and communication along the Indus River Valley to the coast, from which boats would sail to Southeast Asia, Mesopotamia, the Arabian Peninsula, and East Africa.[27] The river was particularly useful for the transport of bulky and fragile commodities. Access to the Arabian Sea was along a coast much further inland during the third and second millennia BCE than the salty marshlands of the Ranns of Kutch in the present day.[28]

Land routes connected the city north and west to the Iranian plateau and Central Asia, and even further north and west to the Near East. Kulli-Mehi ceramics from the hill villages of the Indus period have been found in archaeological sites as far as Mesopotamia and even Syria. Carnelian beads and seals inscribed with their untranslatable language have been discovered at the Royal Cemetery at Ur, dating from the Kassite period (approximately 1500-1155 BCE).[29] By the second millennium BCE crops native to Africa were being seen in the Indus Valley, though it is unclear if these came gradually eastwards along the sea- and land-based trade routes, or if instead Indus traders themselves went as far as Oman and Africa and returned to the Indus heartland with seeds.[30]

The Indus people of Mohenjo-daro were ingenious hydraulic engineers. Each house had access to a "bathroom", which most frequently consisted of a gently sloping platform leading to a drain and an adjacent lavatory. An intricate drainage system was then used to channel the population's sewage and waste water, which was led into conduits that would bring it far from the settlement's perimeter.[31] This horizontal system of conduits existed below the entire city, channeling waste from homes along flat-based conduits half a meter below the street surface. Cesspits and vertical soakage jars, also known as "sumps", were installed at regular points along the conduits, and they may have prevented the waste of clean water by separating dirty water from waste sludge to be recycled in the drainage channels. These were also useful as storm-drains during the monsoon seasons, preventing the discharge of human waste onto the streets. The conduits possibly discharged into the Indus River, or into an area to the west of the high artificial platform, as indicated by the lack of urban development there.[32]

According to archaeological evidence, all of this was built by masons with such skill that there must have been almost no leaks. These were so effective because of their particular shape and size, the materials used and skill with which they were installed, their gently sloping gradient, and the regular supply of a large volume of recycled water to flush the waste at great speed. Similarly efficient and complex drainage systems have been found in other cities of the Indus

---

[27] Wright, 2010
[28] McIntosh, 2008
[29] *ibid*
[30] *ibid*
[31] Ratnagar, S. (2014) "The drainage systems at MohenjoDaro and Nausharo: A technological breakthrough or a stinking disaster?" *Studies in People's History*, 1:1. 1-6
[32] Wheeler, 1953

Civilization, such as the network of ceramic pipes at Nausharo.[33]

More than 700 cylindrical sinking wells made of modified wedge-shaped bricks with narrow openings were built around the city, distributed in such a way that meant almost every house had access to fresh water. As the city grew and new buildings were built upon the remains of previous structures, accumulated layers of debris caused each new structure to be built slightly higher from that which came before. Because of this, wells had to be constantly heightened – resulting in staggeringly tall shafts of up to 20 meters tall.

[33] Jarrige, C. (2000) "The mature Indus phase at Nausharo". In M. Taddei and G. de Marco (eds) *South Asian Archaeology*. Rome. 237–58.

M.Bastle Ullah's picture of a tall well at the site

Another well outside Mohenjo-daro

Bathing and cleanliness appear to have been highly valued amongst the people of Mohenjo-daro. The supply of water may have been particularly revered in ways other than merely functional, with ritual cleansing an important part of daily life. The small bathhouse at the top of the western stairs suggests that cleanliness was a factor considered in the control of access to the

69

citadel. This, and other examples, gives present-day researchers a rare glimpse into how social hierarchies were implemented in Indus societies.

Enormous amounts of labor would have been required to build and maintain the mudbrick structures of the city, especially during the formative years of the settlement but also continuously throughout its entire occupation in response to natural weathering and wear and tear. It is estimated that the city would have required around four million man-days for its initial construction.[34] This alone implies that some form of centralized administrative power existed, and that it organized labor and controlled the means of city-wide construction projects, at least in terms of managing skilled and unskilled laborers and the supply of raw materials. Political power in Mohenjo-daro may therefore have been centered on controlling the supply of labor, acquisition of resources, and craft production.

Power and control would also have been entangled in the acquisition and use of symbolically prestigious objects made of expensive raw materials. The same routes that were used for moving and trading commodities would likely also have been used for communication between the major Indus cities. This would have facilitated the adoption of standardized ideologies, for example between the alleged "twin capitals" of Mohenjo-daro and Harappa. Luxury goods were made of increasingly rare and exotic materials, using techniques that were more specialized than ever before. Moreover, since there is still no evidence of a monetary system, grain might have been the most important commodity in the city, with the acquisition and redistribution of wheat and barley as taxes and tithes via state-run granaries being a tightly controlled affair. This would have required an extensive body of administrative staff; it might have been these who made use of the inscribed steatite seals and copper tablets to conduct their affairs.

An open society has less control, whereas a hierarchical society has more, and the complex layout of the urban landscape at Mohenjo-daro suggests areas of spatial inclusion and exclusion. Rather than being used defensively, recent academic studies have argued that the walls, ramps, staircases, monumental access points, complicated floor plans, and platform elevation were all features of the landscape used to spatially manage social relations. Space enables the control of social encounters, and the manipulation of the city's layout was used to direct people along certain paths and to heighten their awareness, intensify their experience of awe, and segregate access. Gates and walls may have been used to separate and control access to the ceremonial or political complex of the citadel from the residential parts of the city. Even within the citadel movement may have been controlled, to separate the areas of daily activity of the permanent residents from temporary visitors to the site.[35] A small gate and flight of stairs on the western edge of the citadel platform could have restricted access to the northern half of the precinct, as may have a gateway extending between the Great Bath and the College Square.

---

[34] McIntosh, 2008

[35] Atre, S. (1987) *The Archetypal Mother: a systemic approach to Harappan religion*. Pune: Ravish Publishers

If this was the reason for the layout, it remains unknown by what criteria social divisions were made: sex, rank, class, kin, occupation, or age. These may also have been simply used to channel merchants and to collect taxes on goods entering and leaving the city.[36] Even in the lower city the differentiation between groups is indicated by the archaeological remains. Platforms could have served as a means to symbolically differentiate between the houses of local elites, the common and low status groups of the city, and those visiting from the outside.

Early interpretations of this part of the upper city were that it was some kind of cultic landscape used by a priestly class. If this was true, the hardship of regular daily movement around the topographically-challenging landscape would certainly have been a significant part of the worshiper's bodily experience. The anticipation of the traveler climbing the rock-cut staircase leading from the settlement to the forecourt of the Great Bath or College Square would have been accentuated by the monumental architecture and expensive building materials surrounding them. Likewise, travelers crossing the flatlands of the Indus River Valley would have been struck by the formidable sight of the monumental citadel.

It is unknown if differences existed in human burial practices amongst the elite and non-elite groups of Mohenjo-daro, as to this day no cemetery has been discovered at the city, nor have individual graves or tombs showing ostentatious displays of luxury material wealth. Less than 40 skeletons that can be dated to the time of the Indus Valley Civilization have been discovered in Mohenjo-daro.[37] Many were disarticulated and incomplete human remains haphazardly and seemingly irreverently buried in contorted positions.

At Mohenjo-daro a great variety and amount of games-related artifacts have been discovered, giving a rare perspective into the third millennium BCE's perspective on the concepts of "fun" and "games", in addition to the lives of children in the city.[38] Archaeological projects have revealed evidence of various types of dice and gaming figures across the Indus Valley. Gaming boards have also been found, with designs ranging from a grid of concentric squares to boards with separate rectangular compartments for the gaming pieces. At Mohenjo-daro, the most popular game-related artifacts were hollow round objects that rattle when shaken, cube-shaped dice made of pottery, and spheres made of marble, shell, and stone. In addition, there were anthropomorphic and zoological figurines made of faience, terra cotta, stone, and unbaked clay, and others "gamesmen" in the shape of tetrahedrons and fish. So-called "casting bones" were carved from ivory and bone, and unlike knuckle bones were decorated in a similar manner to dice. Other, undecorated "sticks" of ivory may also have been used for gaming.

There are many debates regarding the significance of these artifacts for Indus society; some maintain that they were purely used as an entertaining pastime, while others argue that they held

---

[36] Kenoyer, 2000
[37] Dales, G.F. (2006) *The Mythical Massacre at Mohenjo-daro*. University of Pennsylvania: ProQuest
[38] Rogersdotter, E. (2011) *Gaming in Mohenjo-daro – an Archaeology of Unities*. Göteborg: University of Gothenburg

ritual significance.[39] It is also unknown if these games were indigenous to the Indus Civilization or if they were appropriated from other cultures. Comparisons have been made with strikingly similar games pieces and boards from contemporary Iran and Mesopotamia, and in particular those found in Ur and Shahr-i Sokhta.[40]

Late Harappan Harappa

The Late Harappan phase of the Indus Valley Civilization, often referred to as the Post-Urban Harappan, began sometime around 1900 BCE. This phase is generally marked by a lack of creativity throughout the Indus Valley and a decline in urban life, so much so that by 1700 BCE little remained of the Harappan culture. By 1500, the once great cities were all gone. In fact, Harappa became so depopulated during this period that it could no longer be considered a city, but more of a settlement where the cemetery was the most important feature (Possehl 2002, 237).

The decline happened gradually, and there are very few signs of a sudden invasion as was once believed (Avari 2007, 52). Some Indus Valley cities did better than others during this period, and Harappa was actually one of the more enduring, but even Harappa not stave off the decay permanently.

The archaeological evidence from Late Harappan Harappa shows a city in transition in almost every way, even as it does not suggest what exactly drove that transition. Among the features of Late Harappan Harappa, Cemetery H has was one of the most prominent. Cemetery H is located adjacent to Cemetery R37, just to its north, between that cemetery and Mound AB, and researchers have determined it was the cemetery for Late Harappan Harappa (Possehl 2002, 66). It appears that Cemetery H was created long after Cemetery R37 had fallen out of use, and considering the time that elapsed between periods, there is a chance that the Harappans of the Late Harappan phase did not even know about Cemetery R37. The Harappans around 1900 BCE, though, probably did know about Cemetery R37 and thus decided to build the new cemetery next to it. Again, more knowledge of the ancient Indus Valley religion would help scholars determine if the reason for building Cemetery H next to Cemetery R37 was done out of convenience or if there were religious and spiritual implications. The excavations of Cemetery H have revealed that it is different in many ways from Cemetery R37, suggesting a possible shift in religious ideology.

Furthermore, there are noticeable differences within the cemetery to the point where it was practically two different cemeteries.

---

[39] Kenoyer, 2000
[40] Finkel, I. L. (1999) "The Sedentary Games of India: An Introduction". In N. Ray and A. Ghosh (eds) *Sedentary Games of India*. Calcutta: The Asiatic Society. 1-21

Cemetery H is comprised of two very different strata. Stratum II consists of burials that differed in terms of content in the eastern and western parts of the cemetery. The burials in the eastern part of the cemetery were generally complete burials, while those in the west were incomplete. The people were almost always interred in the eastern portion of Cemetery H were buried supine, primarily in an east-west orientation, although northeast-southeast and one example of west-east were also found (Possehl 2002, 170). Since none were interred in a north-south orientation as they were in Cemetery R37, scholars are trying to determine why there was a difference. It may simply be that the burial orientations began in an east-west orientation for no particular reason, and then continued that way due to space and expediency, but that would also raise questions about why the burials in Cemetery R37 were orientated as they were. If the bodies were orientated in Cemetery R37 for religious reasons as was suggested earlier, then the differences in Cemetery H may represent a religious change. Perhaps the Harappans changed their primary deity during the transition from the Mature to the Late Harappan phase, or maybe the concept of the afterlife evolved, and people may have become more cynical and placed less emphasis on things that once mattered more in earlier periods.

It may never be known why the orientation of the burials was different in Cemetery H than in Cemetery R37, but even more interesting is the change that happened during the Late Harappan phase in Cemetery H. Stratum II of Cemetery H, which is above stratum I archaeologically speaking and therefore was a later development, is quite different than stratum I. The burials of stratum I are located in both the eastern and western sections of the cemetery and consist of pottery/burial urns containing human bones. Some of these urns also contained animal bones, although it appears that in some cases the rodent bones may have come from the animals burrowing into the pots after they were buried. Many of the pots contain the remains of more than one individual, leading to the possibility that they were gathered from a mass burial location and then placed in the pots (Possehl 2002, 171). Biological examinations of the remains from Harappa cemeteries indicate that the people buried in Cemetery R37 and stratum II of Cemetery H were similar, but that both of those groups are different from stratum I of Cemetery H (Possehl 2002, 171). The biological evidence, combined with the difference in burial style, seems to indicate that a different ethnic group was living in Harappa by 1700 BCE. What this means for understanding how ancient Harappan society declined remains to be seen, but it certainly raises a number of interesting possibilities.

The majority of civic activity in Late Harappan Harappa appears to have taken place on what is referred to as Mound AB. Mound AB was first excavated by Wheeler in 1947 and has since had other occasional work done (Kenoyer 1991, 35). Mound AB is located adjacent to and north of Cemetery H, adjacent and west-northwest of Mound E, and adjacent and south of Mound F. Some civic activity continued on Mound F in the Late Harappan phase, but activity appears to have gradually come to an end on Mound E (Kenoyer 1991, 56). The archaeological evidence shows that general maintenance of the city began to decline in the later Mature Harappan phase, which resulted in garbage accumulation and eventually most people moving to what is now

Mound AB (Kenoyer 1991, 57). By all accounts, it looks like the people continued their culture for some time and lived on Mound AB as they did in the earlier parts of Harappa. A large well has been excavated on Mound AB as well as a habitation style that was found on Mound F. The Mound F habitation style that was duplicated on Mound AB involved large houses surrounded by smaller ones. Kenoyer believed that this was probably part of a larger workmen's quarter (Kenoyer 1991, 34).

Wheeler discovered remnants of walls around Mound AB, and what he thought was a gateway on the western side (Kenoyer 1991, 35). No major structures have been discovered on Mound AB, such as the granary, and determinations of dating some areas of the mound have been confusing due to some building activity there left over the Early Harappan phase (Kenoyer 1991, 38). The gateway on Mound AB would suggest that, like the similar structure on Mound E, trade was still important at Harappa, at least in the early Late Harappan phase, but the excavations do reveal that Harappa, like the Indus Valley Civilization in general, was in a period of full decline in the Late Harappan phase.

At Harappa, Kenoyer argued that the archaeological evidence indicates the decline was due to changing settlement patterns and nothing nefarious (Kenoyer 1991, 56). There are no burn layers, which are usually found in cities destroyed by warfare, nor have there been any significant numbers of weapons discovered at Harappa. Thus, instead of Harappa being destroyed by the invading Aryans, its collapse may be simpler than experts formerly thought. Kenoyer pointed out that the garbage accumulation on Mound E and evidence of general congestion throughout the city in the late Mature Harappan and Late Harappan phases demonstrates that the city leaders, whoever they were, lost civic control (Kenoyer 1991, 57). Once an elite ruling class begins to lose authority over its population, the road to collapse is not far behind. A state's economy, in ancient as well as modern societies, is often based on the authority of that same state, so if the people no longer respect the authority, the merchants will go elsewhere.

Without adequate funding coming in from the far-flung trade networks, it was only a matter of time until the garbage began accumulating and the once prized drainage system of Harappa became overwhelmed. Eventually, the people left the city, as well as the other Indus Valley cities, and returned to a more agrarian based life.

The Modern Discovery of Kalibangan

The remains of Kalibangan remained under modern fields and settlements well into the 20th century, unlike the major Indus cities, which were already being excavated decades earlier. Nonetheless, modern knowledge of artifacts from Kalibangan predated its discovery and the identification of the Harappan Civilization.

September 24, 1924 is generally viewed as the precise date when the modern discovery of the

Harappan Civilization occurred and research began. Although the major Indus cities had been discovered before that time, scholars did not yet know what they had in front of them and thus were unaware the Harappan Civilization existed as a unique culture that predated all others in India. It was on that date in 1924 that British scholar John Marshall announced the discovery of Mohenjo-daro and Harappa in the *Illustrated London News*. Marshall was convinced that these two cities represented a phase in Indian civilization that predated the Vedic Period, and that many more Bronze Age cities were waiting to be discovered beneath the modern settlements and fields of India. A week later, Assyriologist and Near Eastern archaeologist A.H. Sayce confirmed Marshall's periodization of Mohenjo-daro and Harappa by noting the existence of Indus seals in Bronze Age Mesopotamia (Possehl 2002, 3). The confirmation led to archaeologists fanning out across the Indus Valley to look for more lost Harappan cities. Evidence pointing to the existence of some of these cities, including Kalibangan, had already been circulating throughout academia.

Some excellent examples of Kalibangan pottery had reached markets in Delhi and Bombay in the 19th century, where they were bought by British citizens and eventually ended up in British museums and universities. Some of those pieces were published in academic journals in the late 19th century, but the authors did not know of their origin or even the existence of Kalibangan (Possehl 2002, 3). It would not be until the late 1950s, after India had attained independence, that interest in Kalibangan attracted archaeologists.

The British may have led the way in late 19th century and early 20th century Indology, but native Indian academics took over Harappan archaeology after Indian independence in 1947. The site of Kalibangan was identified in the late 1950s, and excavations by the Archaeological Survey of India began in the 1960-1961 season, led by B.B. Lal and B.K. Thapar. The two archaeologists worked for a total of nine seasons until the 1968-1969 season, although they were forced to occasionally suspend operations due to the extreme heat of the Thar desert.

Kalibangan proved to be a boon to Indus Valley archaeology since there was relatively little modern development on top of the site, which allowed the archaeologists to conduct a complete horizontal excavation. In fact, the work at Kalibangan marked the first horizontal excavation of an Indus site, which helped to explain much about life throughout the Indus Valley Civilization (Possehl 2002, 20).

The focus of many archaeological digs tends to be on the monuments, houses, temples, and other large structures, which was also the case at Kalibangan. The fire pits, streets, and cemetery help partially tell the story about how the people of the city lived and what they believed, but a lot of information can also come from some of the smaller items discovered, as well as the notable absence of certain items. For example, pottery and smaller items can often indicate more about the lives of non-elites, such as the different social groups and professions that were present at a specific site.

Among the various pots and pottery shards excavated at Kalibangan were several tools made of terracotta. Although terracotta has been primarily used throughout history for statuary and art, this ceramic style was used for building tools at Kalibangan. Length scales, hourglasses and plumb-bobs were all tools that have been unearthed in various parts of the site, and while the tools may not have been as sturdy as those made from copper or bronze, they were strong enough to get the job done and were just as sophisticated and accurate. Along with the terracotta tools, several pans that were used for balances and a number of weights made of chert and agate were discovered (Balasubramaniam and Joshi 2008, 588). An examination of the tools discovered at Kalibangan has led historians to conclude that the Harappan people developed advanced and accurate scales and measurements - in fact, it has even been determined that the standard unit of measure in the Indus Valley was 17.63 millimeters. (Balasubramaniam and Joshi 2008, 89).

The existence of these tools also demonstrates that the Harappan people were industrious and skilled, which explains how they were able to plot out and build streets with such precision. The tools were also used to build the many houses and the baths in Kalibangan. The existence of these relatively sophisticated tools also shows that there was a skilled artisan class at Kalibangan.

The absence of other materials also says much about the people of Kalibangan. Most notably, weapons are almost entirely absent from the site, a stark contrast to Bronze Age sites in Mesopotamia and Egypt from the same time period that have routinely produced various weapons, both ceremonial and practical. Outside of the evidence of human destruction at a number of late Early Harappan sites, there is relatively little evidence of warfare in Harappan society and virtually none from Kalibangan. This may have set the precedent somewhat for art in later periods of Indian civilization, as depictions of warfare were nearly absent, unlike the art of Egypt and Mesopotamia, where the kings were routinely depicted as virile warriors (Kenoyer 1999, 82). The absence of weaponry does not necessarily mean that the Harappans were pacifists, but it does seem to suggest that warfare played a far less important role in their society compared to other ancient cultures.

Written texts were also in short supply in Kalibangan. Many of the examples of writing recovered from the Indus Valley were found on cylindrical terracotta or faience tablets, and the writing on the tablets consisted of short inscriptions yet to be deciphered. The Harappan people also made copper tablets, but none of those have been recovered from Kalibangan and only a couple of the terracotta tablets were excavated in the city (Kenoyer 1999, 74). It is tempting to draw conclusions from the dearth of written texts recovered from Kalibangan, but to do so without more evidence would be problematic. Without knowing more about the Harappan language, it would be guesswork to speculate over why there were so few written texts recovered from Kalibangan. It should be pointed out that although there were very few written texts found at Kalibangan, a number of stamp seals were discovered at the site. Seals depicting unicorns, zebus, and centaurs were all found among the ruins of ancient Kalibangan (Possehl 2002, 76). As mentioned earlier, the mythical creatures on the Kalibangan seals may be related to Harappan religion, but it is difficult to say for sure.

Outside of the Aryans in the middle of the second millennium BCE, none of the many groups gained ascendency over the others on the Indian subcontinent. That situation would not change until the late 4ᵗʰ century BCE, when a Macedonian king managed to lead his army all the way to the banks of the Indus River on his way to conquering much of the known world.

India proved to be more vast than Alexander the Great ever imagined, and far from the end of the world. His army crossed the Punjab, but upon reaching the Hyphasis, or the modern Beas River, his men would march no further. Alexander raged, begged, entreated, and even threatened, but his soldiers had had enough. Further east lay still more powerful Indian kingdoms who, rumor had it, would await them on the eastern bank of the mighty river Ganges with hundreds of thousands of cavalry and infantry, and thousands of war elephants and charioteers besides. Alexander flew into a black rage, refusing all visitors for days, but eventually he relented, realizing that no matter how great their love for him might be, he could not persuade his veterans to march further south. After erecting a monument on the Hyphasis River to mark the easternmost edge, he at last turned his army westwards for the first time in almost 10 years.

Alexander's Indian campaign is important because of the light that it sheds on the history of a region that was previously obscure, at least to people in Europe. He influenced the cultural history of the Indus Valley by introducing Greek culture, but even though he briefly garrisoned India and brought it under the administrative control of his empire, his successors were unable to retain control of it for very long. Within a few centuries, India would be as distant and mysterious to the Romans as it had been to the Greeks.

The Loss and Rediscovery of Mohenjo-daro

The Indus Civilization can be described as having gone through three main phases: expansion, integration, and collapse. Naturally, there is much speculation, and many theories, focused on the last of these stages. At some point during the Post-Urban/Jhukar Period (approximately 1900-1700 BCE), the Indus Civilization underwent a remarkable transformation, as the major urban centers were abandoned and their populations disappeared.[41] This occurred at Mohenjo-daro as well, though research in the past decade has shown that this was not nearly as rapid as previously believed.

The most dramatic and frequently mentioned theory was proposed by R.P. Chanda, an associate of one of the earliest archaeologists of the city, Sir John Marshall. Chanda believed that the Vedic Indo-Aryans destroyed the cities and massacred the people of the Indus Civilization, based on human remains he found that had been unceremoniously discarded on the streets or in the ruined houses of Mohenjo-daro from the final period of its occupation. The Aryans were an Indo-European people that came to the Indian subcontinent from its northern borders sometime during the second millennium BCE. They allegedly used chariots driven by horses raised on the

---

[41] Wright, 2010

Eurasian steppe, and armed themselves with the latest military innovations: bows, arrows, javelins, axes, and swords.[42] According to this side of the story, the city's men, women, and children were massacred at the hands of Aryan invaders, leaving the streets of city littered with corpses after the population was totally exterminated. Human remains were used to give legitimacy to the massacre myth, such as the incomplete skeleton found on the so-called "Deadman's Lane", as were tales of Indra, the principle deity of the Aryans, known also as the "fort-destroyer" for his role in destroying the citadels of the *dasyu* (mortal or supernatural enemies of the Aryans).[43]

Chanda

However, there is a lack of material evidence that attests to destruction of this scale having ever taken place. The lack of weapons, human remains, or damage to buildings from this period – indeed, the lack of violence indicated in any period of Indus history – suggest that the residents of Mohenjo-daro were a distinctly unwarlike people. No human remains have been found in the fortified citadel, which would have likely been where much of the fighting would have occurred if such an invasion occurred. Moreover, the human remains used to support this story date much later than the Indus Valley Civilization period; most of them are from later burials that had cut

---

[42] Dales, 2006
[43] *ibid*

through the archaeological layers of the city.[44]

The chronology that has been established through continued archaeological work in the last two centuries indicates that such an invasion simple did not take place, and the "massacre" at Mohenjo-daro never occurred. Instead, a series of human and natural factors contributed to the general deterioration of the Indus Valley Civilization and the abandonment of Mohenjo-daro. The region was and is still tectonically active, as the Himalayas are pushed upwards by the forces of continental drift, causing the collision of the Indian and Eurasian tectonic plates. This convergent continental-continental boundary leads to a number of devastating results, including earthquakes and land shifts. This means that the entire area is continuously rising, and even slight changes to the region's topography can have an enormous impact on drainage. For example, archaeological remote-sensing and geophysical surveys carried out at Cholistan, Pakistan, have revealed that at some point during the second millennium BCE the major Saraswati River dried up.[45] This is supported by the earliest Vedic texts of India, which describe a major river in the general area drying up sometime between the early second and first millenniums BCE. Today an arid stretch of ground with small, intermittent rivers known as the Ghaggar-Hakra, during the Indus period this was a powerful watercourse whose loss must have had devastating repercussions for farmers who relied upon its annual floods.

Climate may have been a factor in the environmental degradation and major demographic upheavals of the region. Floods were already common in the Indus River Valley, but analysis of pollen remains recovered by archaeologists has indicated that rainfall rose steadily during the third millennium BCE and declined considerably during the second millennium.[46] This climate change had an impact on the vegetation of the region, as analysis shows that during this period deciduous forests were replaced by shorter thorn trees known to thrive only in dry soil with poor water retention.[47] At the same time, there was a general deterioration in the maintenance of buildings and dams in the city. These changes would have increased the amount of water that was draining into the Indus River, causing it to flow faster and increasing the likelihood of floods.

Since the second millennium BCE the Indus River has shifted more than two kilometers from its original location.[48] As the Indus River crept gradually closer to Mohenjo-daro, the greater frequency and force of the floods would have been of great concern for the city's residents. A similar entanglement of natural and cultural attributes causing landscape change occurred in contemporary Mesopotamia, where the flat flood plain caused the Tigris and Euphrates rivers to shift often and quickly, causing sudden changes to settlement patterns.

---

[44] *ibid*
[45] McIntosh, 2008
[46] *ibid*
[47] *ibid*
[48] Jansen, M. (1986) *Die Indus-Zivilisation: Wiederentdeckung einer frühen Hochkultur*. Köln: DuMont Buchverlag

The water table near Mohenjo-daro rose as a result of these changing environmental conditions. This would have led to increased levels of soil salinity, and in turn that must have had a detrimental impact on agricultural yields.[49] Farms in the hinterland could not sustainably provide enough food for the city's population, leading to overgrazing and deforestation – each of which only exacerbated the problem. Deforestation was also caused by the enormous fuel requirements of the mid brick industry and for the copper industries of the city. Vast amounts of charcoal would have been required to reach the temperatures required to manufacture these bricks, and in the second millennium BCE animal dung was being used instead of charcoal, indicating that there was not enough wood available in the city's hinterland.[50]

Finally, changing trade routes may have also played a role in the city's decline. Land-based trade appears to have been replaced by a reliance on maritime trade by the end of the third millennium BCE, but the sudden rise in the Arabian Sea coastline of West Pakistan in the second millennium BCE might have disrupted these sea-based links during the period of Mohenjo-daro's deterioration.[51]

Living standards in Mohenjo-daro declined massively and irreversibly as a result of these changing conditions. The structural integrity of later houses, with thin and poorly assembled walls, was far worse than the solid, mud-brick buildings of the third millennium. Many of the monumental buildings were divided up and converted into other functions, such as pottery kilns and workshops. There appears to have been a sudden surge in population within the city limits, followed by a sudden depopulation of the entire settlement and suburban landscape.[52] The Great Bath and other large buildings fell out of use, and archaeological remains even indicate that deadly diseases were rife during this period of deterioration, including malaria and cholera.

These diverse factors eventually led to large-scale population migrations southeast, and the growth of settlements in the Kathiawar peninsula, north of present-day Bombay.[53] Surveys at Gujarat have shown that significant growth in the number of settlements took place between 2000 and 1800 BCE. South of the Punjab, the Ganges Valley became the focal point of civilizational growth. Writing, urban settlement patterns, centralized control, international trade, occupational specialization, and widely distributed standardized artifacts all changed during this process, each fragmenting into regionally distinctive forms. Immediately after the abandonment of Mohenjo-daro, the city became a hotbed of banditry as raiders from the Baluchistan hills occupied the ruins.[54]

At some point during the 2nd century CE a Buddhist stupa and monastery were built upon the

---

[49] McIntosh, 2008
[50] *ibid*
[51] Jansen, 2002
[52] McIntosh, 2008
[53] Dales, 2006
[54] *ibid*

former citadel. However, there is a dearth of research that focuses on the later uses of Mohenjo-daro, even though it was an interest in these Buddhist ruins that first led archaeologists to the site, and thus the discovery of Mohenjo-daro's prehistoric past.

The earliest European visitors to India came during the 16th and 17th centuries CE. Of these, only a few took an interest in the ruins of the Indus River Valley; most were chasing semi-mythological landscapes described in ancient Indian literature.[55] The Sanskrit *Rig-Veda* is the oldest known text from India, a collection of "Vedic" hymns compiled into 10 books which describe the deities and cosmological views of the people in the Punjab during the mid-second millennium BCE. The *Ramayana* – also written in Sanskrit – is another text of great antiquity. This mythological epic may have been written at around the turn of the Common Era, and though later than the Indus period it attracted the attention of European explorers eager to learn more about the lands in which it was based.

These antiquarians were good observers of the landscape, but poor interpreters of it, and it was only during the 18th century that an interest in Indian antiquities began to pick up, mostly driven by an interest in discovering unknown Buddhist ruins. In 1784, the Asiatic Society of Bengal was founded by the London-born philologist Sir William Jones, who would later be the first person to propose the existence of the Indo-European family of languages. In 1871 Alexander Cunningham became director-general of the Archaeological Survey of India. Cunningham had visited Harappa in the 1850s, but when he returned in the 1870s to investigate the site he found the ruins had been largely damaged by laborers who were using the ancient mud bricks to construct a railroad traversing the area.[56] Other surveys were undertaken by W. T. Blanford, who found Indus remains in the Rohri Hills in 1875 and again at Sutkagen-dor two years later.[57]

[55] Urban, G. (1991) "The Indus Civilization: the Story of a Discovery". In M. Jansen, M. Mulloy and G. Urban (eds) *Forgotten Cities on the Indus: Early Civilization in Pakistan from the 8th to the 2nd Millennium BC*. Mainz: Philipp von Zabern. 18-26.
[56] McIntosh, 2008
[57] *ibid*

Cunningham

Up to the late 19th century, most academics believed that civilizations and complex urban societies only appeared in India during the first millennium BCE, but this picture changed during the 20th century, when excavations at Mohenjo-daro were performed by some of the most famous names in the history of archaeology. Archaeologists working with the Archaeological Survey of India began investigating the site from the 1920s. Rai Bahadur Daya Ram Sahni and Rakal Das Banerji were some of the earliest, but the ancient city only came to international attention through the work of Sir John Marshall and Ernest Mackay. Marshall was attracted to Mohenjo-daro by the presence of the Buddhist monastic ruins at the summit of the conspicuous mound, and in 1922 he began excavating the site. As he bored through the extremely deep layers of mud bricks he became the first to discover that the mound was man-made, and one of the earliest to realize the great antiquity of the site by dating the site to before the Mauryan period (322 – 185 BCE). Marshall returned to Mohenjo-daro four more times between 1925 and 1927, and through these projects came to the conclusion that the Indus civilization was India's "indigenous" civilization.

Ernest John Henry Mackay was the next archaeologist to visit Mohenjo-daro, employed by Marshall in 1926 to continue the excavations on a full time basis.[58] He discovered human

---

[58] Possehl, 2002

remains lying on the streets of the uppermost periods of occupation, which were used to support R. P. Chanda's hypothesis regarding the Aryan invasion of the city. Together, the results of Marshall and Mackay formed the foundation for almost all subsequent research of the settlement.

Mackay

Between 1925 and 1926 Marshall employed more than a thousand laborers for the large-scale excavations of the site.[59] However, by 1931, problems with funding meant that large-scale excavations had to be abandoned, though some smaller-scale projects were undertaken by Q. M. Moneer and Puri in 1932-1933 and 1935-36 and by A. Rahman in 1938. It was during this time that connections were being made between Mohenjo-daro and Harappa. The renowned Australian archaeologist Gordon Childe took an interest in the debate, and in the 1930s he proposed a set of key identifying features of the Indus Civilization: their complex drainage systems, absence of palatial, religious, or mortuary structures, a competent bureaucracy, the lack of evidence suggesting their engagement in military activity, and a unifying ideology reified by the striking similarities between their cities. His checklist of attributes has been applied to Indus settlements ever since.

The British archaeologist and Director General of the Archaeological Survey of India, Sir R.E. Mortimer Wheeler, frequented Mohenjo-daro following the partition of Pakistan from India in 1947. As advisor for the Pakistan government on matters of archaeology he carried out three excavations on the site in 1950, during which he discovered the "Great Granary".

Most interest in Mohenjo-daro and the Indus Civilization up to the mid-20th century was culture historical in approach. Compared to other modes of explaining society, culture history gives relatively little concern over questions about how societies work. Instead, it focuses on

---

[59] Marshall, J. (ed.) (1931) *Mohenjo-daro and the Indus Civilization: Being an official account of Archaeological Excavations at Mohenjo-daro carried out by the Government of India between the years 1922 and 1927. Vol. I-III*. London: Arthur Probsthain.

identifying a succession and diffusion of different cultures, which change due to external causes, such as conquest and migration. The "evolution" and "devolution" of the Indus Civilization was of primary interest to the British archaeologist Stuart Piggott during his investigations of the Zhob and Quetta cultures.[60] Normative approaches to archaeology prevailed; it was believed that "culture" was simply expressed through the artifacts and cities of the Indus people and could be interpreted through these material remains.

The final season of these initial excavations at Mohenjo-daro were carried out by Dr. George F. Dales, between 1964 and 1965. At this time, Anglo-American archaeologists were becoming increasingly dissatisfied with culture historical approaches. Emphasis was increasingly placed on asking questions of why the Indus Valley Civilization flourished and did what they did, rather than simply identifying who and what the Indus Valley Civilization were. By the 1970s, different research questions and methodologies had drastically changed the management of Mohenjo-daro as a heritage site.

---

[60] Piggott, S. (1950) *Prehistoric India*. London: Pelican. Series

Mamoon Mengal's picture of the "Priest-King" sculpture from the site

Today, the conservation and management of the present-day site falls under the aegis of the government of Pakistan, and in particular the Department of Archaeology. Mohenjo-daro is of such great importance to the nation of Pakistan that it is featured on the front of the 10 Rupee note. It is protected by the 1975 Antiquities Act, the 1978 Excavation and Exploration Rules, and the 1979 Immovable Antiquities Rules and Export of Antiquities Rules, in addition to legislative guidelines provided through its status as a UNESCO World Heritage site.[61] The Indian state has

[61] Director General of the Department of Archaeology and Museums, Government of Pakistan (1980) Nomination Document for the Archaeological Ruins of Moenjodaro

also conducted numerous investigations into its Indus past

UNESCO first sent a mission to Mohenjo-daro in 1972, followed by the creation of a comprehensive report on the site's integrity and significance starting in 1979. Mohenjo-daro was inscribed onto the UNESCO List of World Heritage Sites in 1980. As a World Heritage site following UNESCO's guidelines, intrusive archaeological methods – methods that physically damage the site, such as excavations – are not allowed. Most recent studies have made use of non-intrusive techniques, such as geophysical surveys, architectural studies of standing remains, sampling of ecofacts, and remote sensing via aerial imagery.

Soon after the earliest excavations at Mohenjo-daro, the structural remains of the site began to deteriorate. This was due to a number of factors, most of all problems of salinity, drainage, climate, and a steadily increasing human presence. Salt reactions were caused by the rising water table – a problem that persists from antiquity to this day, and exacerbated by the conveyance of the Sukkur Barrage and its network of canals in 1932. The gradual, but continuous, westward migration of the Indus River also threatens to encroach upon the site. Over time, the city has been almost severed into two parts by the Indus River floods. In response, the banks of the river have been reinforced with spurs and rock armor.

Moisture infiltrates the now-fragile mud brick ruins directly from rainfall, and the unmaintained hydraulic network no longer drains the site. This causes structural distress to the standing remains in the city. Dozens of modern tube wells have been installed around the site, in addition to a pumping station, to help drain the ruins during the wettest seasons of the year. Nonetheless, trapped moisture continues to weaken the walls, while harsh climatic cycles create thermal stresses, producing cracks and other surface decay.

The site has also been intermittently threatened by the growth of violent Islamic extremist groups such as the Taliban in the region during the 21st century, and in particular during war in Afghanistan between 2001 and 2014. The region remains troubled to this day, yet even in times of peace few changes have been made to conserve the structural remains from the effects of a growing number of tourists visiting the site. Mohenjo-daro was visited by more than 50,000 visitors in 2001.

From the 1980s much international research has been conducted at Mohenjo-daro. The earliest excavations at the city made use of techniques that are considered relatively controversial by today's standards. Ongoing projects mainly aim to clarify and corroborate reports from the 18th and early 19th centuries with the material remains visible on the site today, and to make use of the latest archaeological theories and practices. G. Urban and M. Jansen began the first re-evaluations in 1979, leading the "German Research Project Mohenjo-daro" team from Aachen University, and they were followed in 1981 by the "Italian Mission to Mohenjo-daro". A number of rescue-style excavations were required in 1987 and 1989, due to problems caused by the rising water table and oversalination. The joint Pakistan-American Harappa Archaeological Research

Project (HARP) ongoing projects focused on the city of Harappa. They have discovered evidence of a settlement that predates that of the Indus Civilization, from as far back as 3500 BCE.

At Mohenjo-daro, a mere 10 percent of the massive site has been excavated to this day. Surveys and probing have revealed the great size of the settlement, and over the coming century further excavations are hoped to take place in the suburban areas. The lowest layers of the citadel and lower city remain below the high water table, which has meant that the waterlogged earliest levels of the city's past have not yet been excavated.

Archaeological attention is traditionally focused on temporal components, through detailed analyses of stratigraphic relationships to reveal chronological sequences of events in a small area. Artifacts and excavations offer a very small, detailed, focused source of information for a local area. However, by considering the horizontal, spatial components of landscape we can get a much more anthropological view of the past.[62] Recent research has taken a more holistic approach towards situating the city within its landscape context, as distinct from merely looking at the settlement in isolation. Instead of studying towns as isolated micro-features, they are analyzed as part of a regionally integrated macro-system of change. However, it remains unknown what relationships emerged from the range of social actions and motivations of those residing in the city and those living in its immediate hinterland and wider landscape.

Only Mohenjo-daro, Harappa, and Dholavira have been investigated extensively by archaeologists. The cities of Ganweriwala and Rakhigarhi have yet to be surveyed or excavated, and may reveal remarkably fresh perspectives on the Indus Civilization if and when they are. A closer focus is being made on the relationship between Mohenjo-daro and surrounding eco-zones and with other settlements in the wider region, in particular the hilltop communities who did not share the same cultural hegemony of the Indus Civilization.[63] Further questions are being asked regarding the spread of the Indus Civilization into other areas of Eurasia: Iran, Mesopotamia, and Central Asia. Surveying, both intensive and extensive, broadens our view to the entire region. GIS modelling offers the potential to indicate 'natural trade routes' and other relationships with the surrounding landscape by modelling key features of the city's hinterland, including the extensive suburban parts of the urban landscape that have not been fully surveyed. Greater attention has also been placed on making more nuanced interpretations of the spaces and buildings of the city. By identifying multiple scales in the formation and use of space in Indus cities, archaeologist may be able to identify the utilitarian, religious and social concerns of the diverse groups who lived there. Space is socially produced by the various perspectives of multiple groups involved in its formation and maintenance.[64] Theoretical tools, such as access analysis, might be usefully applied to the network of complex buildings, lanes, ramps, and

---

[62] Smith, A.T. (2003) *The Political Landscape: Constellations of Authority in Early Complex Polities*. Berkeley: University of California Press

[63] Sonawane, V. H. & P. Ajithprasad (1994) "Harappa Culture and Gujarat." *Man and Environment* 19. 129-139.

[64] Tilley, C. (1994) *A phenomenology of landscape : places, paths, and monuments*. Oxford: Berg.

87

gateways found in the city.

There are countless unanswered questions when it comes to the Indus Valley Civilization, and historians hope to answer many of them over the coming years. How will their script be deciphered, and what kind of information will be revealed from Indus textual sources? Archaeologists have recovered a great number of inscribed seals in an unknown language at Mohenjo-daro and other Indus settlements. By the mid-19th century the major Indo-Aryan languages of the region's recent history – Brahmi and Kharoshthi – had been deciphered, but the Indus script and language have remained undecipherable to this day, leading some to suggest that their symbols may not actually be a script.[65] Where exactly did the Indus people come from, and where did they go? What exists directly below the Buddhist stupa – a structure that is positioned atop the most prominent area of the entire city, which to this day has not been excavated? Research has presented few conclusive and many controversial theories concerning the administration and elite classes of the city. Similarly, almost nothing is known about Indus cosmological and religious ideologies and practices - was religion separate from other social phenomena such as gender and identity, or was it a core component of social organization and human relationships?

Moving forward, plenty is known, but much is left to be answered. Neither the emergence nor disappearance of the Indus Valley Civilization was as sudden and dramatic as has been previously believed. They gradually developed a highly complex and bureaucratic urban society over a period of one hundred years – though the preceding circumstances and processes by which this was done remain to be discovered. Likewise, instead of a collapse or massacre, the Indus heartland was gradually depopulated at the beginning of the second millennium BCE. Rather than barbarian invaders, the forces of nature proved to be their foremost enemy, as people emigrated and settled in different areas of the Indian subcontinent to escape from cities that were becoming less able to withstand the erosive effects of climate change.

Further archaeological investigations in the coming century will surely change the current understanding of Mohenjo-daro and wider Indus society; even if it is likely that new discoveries will only lead to further questions and intriguing theories. Today only foundations remain, but the site's importance is represented by its UNESCO World Heritage status, awarded in 1980 for being a site of outstanding cultural importance to the common heritage of humanity.

Online Resources

Other Indian history titles by Charles River Editors

Other titles about India on Amazon

Other titles about Harappa on Amazon

---

[65] McIntosh, 2008

Bibliography

Avari, Burjor. 2007. *India: The Ancient Past: A History of the Indian Sub-continent from c.7000 BC to AD 1200*. London: Routledge.

Belcher, William R. 1991. "Fish Resources in an Early Urban Context at Harappa." In *Harappa Excavations 1986–1990: A Multidisciplinary Approach to Third Millennium Urbanism*, edited by Richard W. Meadow, 5–12. Madison, Wisconsin: Prehistory Press.

Bryant, Edwin. 2001. *The Quest for the Origins of Vedic Culture: The Indo-Aryan Migration Debate*. Oxford: Oxford University Press.

Dales, Georg F. 1991. "Some Specialized Ceramic Studies at Harappa." In *Harappa Excavations1986–1990: A Multidisciplinary Approach to Third Millennium Urbanism*, edited by Richard W. Meadow, 29–60. Madison, Wisconsin: Prehistory Press.

Doniger, Wendy, trans. 1981. *The Rig Veda: An Anthology*. London: Penguin.

Haywood, John. 2005. *The Penguin Historical Atlas of Ancient Civilizations*. London: Penguin.

Hemphill, Brian E., John R. Lukacs, and K.A.R. Kennedy. 1991. "Biological Adaptations and Affinities of Bronze Age Harappans." In *Harappa Excavations 1986–1990: A Multidisciplinary Approach to Third Millennium Urbanism*, edited by Richard W. Meadow, 137–182. Madison, Wisconsin: Prehistory Press.

Kenoyer, Jonathan Mark. 1999. *Ancient Cities of the Indus Valley Civilization*. Oxford: Oxford University Press.

———. 1991. "Urban Process in the Indus Tradition: A Preliminary Model from Harappa." In *Harappa Excavations 1986–1990: A Multidisciplinary Approach to Third Millennium Urbanism*, edited by Richard W. Meadow, 29–60. Madison, Wisconsin: Prehistory

Press.

Kuhrt, Amélie. 2010. *The Ancient Near East: c. 3000–330 BC*. 2 vols. London: Routledge.

Meadow, Richard H. 1991. "Faunal Remains and Urbanism at Harappa." In *Harappa Excavations 1986–1990: A Multidisciplinary Approach to Third Millennium Urbanism*, edited by Richard W. Meadow, 5–12. Madison, Wisconsin: Prehistory Press.

Miller, Heather Margaret-Louis. 1991. "Urban Paleoethnobotany at Harappa." In *Harappa Excavations 1986–1990: A Multidisciplinary Approach to Third Millennium Urbanism*, edited by Richard W. Meadow, 5–12. Madison, Wisconsin: Prehistory Press.

Possehl, Gregory L. 2002. *The Indus Civilization: A Contemporary Perspective*. Lanham, Maryland: Altamira Press.

————. 2000-2001. "The Early Harappan Phase." *Bulletin of the Deccan College Post-Graduate and Research Institute* 60/61: 227-241.

————. 1991. "A Short History of Archaeological Discovery at Harappa." In *Harappa Excavations 1986–1990: A Multidisciplinary Approach to Third Millennium Urbanism*, edited by Richard W. Meadow, 5–12. Madison, Wisconsin: Prehistory Press.

Pritchard, James B, ed. 1992. *Ancient Near Eastern Texts Relating to the Old Testament*. 3rd ed. Princeton, New Jersey: Princeton University Press.

Wright, Rita P. 1991. "Patterns of Technology and the Organization of Production at Harappa."In *Harappa Excavations 1986–1990: A Multidisciplinary Approach to Third Millennium Urbanism*, edited by Richard W. Meadow, 5–12. Madison, Wisconsin: Prehistory Press.

Free Books by Charles River Editors

We have brand new titles available for free most days of the week. To see which of our titles are currently free, click on this link.

Discounted Books by Charles River Editors

We have titles at a discount price of just 99 cents everyday. To see which of our titles are currently 99 cents, click on this link.

Made in the USA
Monee, IL
05 October 2020